SEMIOTEXT(E) INTERVENTION SERIES

© 2011 by Tiqqun. Originally published by Éditions La Fabrique in 2009.
This translation © 2011 by Semiotext(e)

Published by Semiotext(e)
2007 Wilshire Blvd., Suite 427, Los Angeles, CA 90057
www.semiotexte.com

Thanks to John Ebert, Marc Lowenthal, and Jason Smith.

Design: Hedi El Kholti

ISBN: 978-1-58435-097-2
Distributed by The MIT Press, Cambridge, Mass.
and London, England
Printed in the United States of America

Tiqqun

This Is Not a Program

Translated by Joshua David Jordan

semiotext(e)
intervention
series □ 7

Contents

10064 7845x

This Is Not a Program

I don't believe that ordinary people think that in the short run there is any risk of a sudden, violent dissolution of the state, of open civil war. What is gaining ground instead is the idea of latent civil war, to borrow a journalistic expression, the idea of a civil war of position that would strip the state of all legitimacy.

— *Terrorisme et démocratie,* Editions Sociales, 1978[1]

Once again, blind experimentation, with no protocol or almost none. (We have been left so little; this may be our chance.) Once again, direct action, sheer destruction, out-and-out confrontation, the refusal of any kind of mediation: those who don't refuse to understand will get no explanation from us. Again, the desire, the plane of consistency of everything that several decades of counterrevolution have repressed. Again, all this: autonomy, punk, riot, orgy, but original, mature, thought out, clear of the petty convolutions of the new.

Through arrogance, "international police" operations, and communiqués declaring permanent victory, a world presented as the only world possible, as the crowning achievement of civilization, has finally been made thoroughly abominable. A world which believed it had completely insulated itself has discovered evil at its core, among its children. A world which celebrated a common new year as a change of millennium has begun to fear for its millennium. A world long settled in the house of catastrophe now warily grasps that the fall of the "socialist bloc" didn't portend its triumph but rather its own ineluctable collapse. A world gorged with the clamors of the end of history, the American century, and the failure of communism is now going to have to *pay* for its frivolity.

In the present paradoxical situation, this world—that is to say, essentially, its police—has constructed for itself a fitting, and fittingly extravagant, enemy. It talks of a Black Bloc, of a "traveling anarchist circus," of a vast conspiracy against civilization. One is reminded of Von Salomon's Germany in *The Outlaws*, a Germany obsessed by the fantasy of a secret organization, the O.C., "which spreads like a cloud loaded with gas" and to which THEY[2] attribute all the dazzling confusion of a reality given over to civil war. "A bad conscience tries to exorcise the power that threatens it. It creates a bogey that it can make faces at and thinks safety is thereby assured."[3] That sounds about right, doesn't it?

Despite the flights of fancy of the imperial police, current events have no strategic legibility. They have no strategic legibility because if they did that would imply something common, something minimally common between us. And that—a common—makes everyone afraid, it makes Bloom[4] turn away, it stuns and strikes dumb because it restores something unequivocal to the very heart of our suspended lives. We have become accustomed to contracts for everything. We have avoided everything resembling a *pact* because a pact cannot be rescinded; it is either respected or broken. And in the end that is the hardest thing to understand: that the effect of a negation depends on the positivity of a common, that our way of saying "I" determines the force with which we say "no." Often we are surprised by the break in historical transmission, a break arising from the fact that for at least fifty years no "parent" has been able to talk about his life to "his" children, to turn his life into history [*histoire*], a history that isn't simply a discontinuum colored with pathetic anecdotes. What has in fact been lost is the ability to establish a communicable relationship between our history and history as such. At the heart of all this is the belief that by renouncing every *singular* existence, by surrendering all purpose, we might finally get a little peace. Blooms believed that it was enough to abandon the battlefield for the war to end. But nothing like that happened. War didn't stop and those who have refused as much now find themselves a bit more *disarmed*, a bit more *disfigured*, than the rest. This is the source of the resentments that now roil in Blooms' bowls and from which springs the insatiable desire to see heads roll, to finger the guilty, to secure a kind of general repentance for all of history past. A redefinition of historical conflict is needed, not intellectually: vitally.

I say *redefinition* because a definition of historical conflict precedes us in which every existence in the pre-imperial period had its part: *the class struggle.* That definition no longer holds. It condemns us to paralysis, bad faith, and empty talk. No war can now be waged, no life lived, in this straightjacket from another age. To continue the struggle today, we will have to scrap the notion of class and with it the whole entourage of certified origins, reassuring sociologisms, identity prostheses. The notion of class is only good for holding like a little bedpan the neuroses, separation, and perpetual recrimination in which THEY have taken such morbid delight in France, in every segment of society, for such a long time. Historical conflict no longer opposes two massive molar heaps, two classes—the exploited and the exploiters, the dominant and dominated, managers and workers— among which, in each individual case, one could differentiate. The front line no longer cuts through the middle of society; it now runs through the middle of each of us, between what makes us a *citizen*, our predicates, and all the rest. It is thus in each of us that war is being waged between imperial socialization and that which already eludes it. A revolutionary process can be set in motion from any point of the biopolitical fabric, from any singular situation, by exposing, even breaking, the line of flight that traverses it. Insofar as such processes, such ruptures, occur, one plane of consistency is common to all of them: that of anti-imperial subversion. "The generality of the struggle specifically derives from the system of power itself, from all the forms in which power is exercised and applied."[5] We have called this plane of consistency the Imaginary Party, so that in its very name the artifice of its nominal and a fortiori political representation is clear. Like every plane of consistency the Imaginary Party is at once already present and yet to be built. Building the Party no longer means building a total organization within which all ethical differences might be set aside for the sake of a common struggle; today, building the Party means *establishing forms-of-life in their difference, intensifying, complicating relations between them, developing as subtly as possible civil war between us*. Because the most formidable stratagem of Empire lies in its throwing everything that opposes it into one ugly heap—of "barbarism," "sects," "terrorism," or "conflicting extremisms"—fighting against Empire essentially means never confusing the conservative segments of the Imaginary Party—libertarian militias, right-wing anarchists, insurrectionary fascists, Qutbist jihadists, ruralist militants—and its revolutionary-experimental segments. Building the Party must therefore no longer be thought of in terms of organization but in terms of *circulation*. In other words, if there is still a "problem of organization," the problem is organizing the circulation within the Party. For only the continuation and intensification of encounters between us can further the process of ethical polarization, can further the building of the Party.

It is true that a passion for history is generally the fate of bodies incapable of *living* the present. Nonetheless, I don't consider it off topic to return to the aporias of the cycle of struggle initiated in the early 1960s now that another cycle has begun. In the pages that follow, numerous references will be made to 1970s Italy. This is not an arbitrary choice. If I weren't afraid of going on too long, I would easily show how what was then at stake in the starkest and most brutal terms largely remains so for us, although today's climate is, for the time being, less extreme. As Guattari wrote in 1978: "Rather than consider Italy as a special case, captivating but all things considered aberrant, shouldn't we in fact seek to shed light on the other, apparently more stable, social, political, and economic situations originating in more secure state power through a reading of the tensions currently at work in that country?"[6] 1970s Italy remains, in every respect, the insurrectional moment *closest to us*. We must start there, not in order to write the history of a past movement, but to hone the weapons for the war currently taking place.

Those of us who provisionally operate in France don't have it easy. It would be absurd to deny that the conditions in which we operate are determined, and even bloody well determined. Beyond the fanaticism for separation which sovereign state education has engrained in bodies and which makes *school* the shameful utopia hammered into every French skull, there is this distrust, this impossible-to-shake distrust of life, of everything that exists *unapologetically.* And there is the retreat from the world—into art, philosophy, the home, food, spirituality, critique—as the exclusive and impracticable line of flight on which the thickening flows of local mortification feed. An umbilical retreat that calls for the omnipresence of the French state, that despotic schoolmaster which now seems even to govern "citizen" protests. Thus the great din of spineless, crippled, and *twisted* French minds, which never stop whirling round within themselves, every second feeling more threatened sensing that something might wake them from their complacent misery.

Nearly everywhere in the world debilitated bodies have some historical icon of resentment on which to cling, some proud fascistoid movement that has decked out in grand style the coat of arms of the reaction.

Nothing doing in France. French conservatism has never had any style, because it is a bourgeois conservatism, a *gut* conservatism. That it has finally risen to the rank of pathological reflexivity changes nothing. It isn't driven by its love for a dying world, but by its terror of experimentation, of life, of life-experimentation. This conservatism, the ethical substratum of specifically French bodies, takes precedence over any kind of political position, over any kind of *discourse*. It establishes the existential continuity, a declared as much as hidden continuity, that ensures that Bové,[7] the 17th arrondissement bourgeois, the pencil pusher of the *Encyclopédie des Nuisances*,[8] and the provincial notable all belong to the *same party*. It matters little, then, that the bodies in question voice reservations about the existing order; the same passion for origins, forests, pastures, and village life is currently on display in opposition to worldwide financial speculation, and tomorrow it will stifle even the smallest movement for revolutionary deterritorialization. Regardless of where, those who speak solely from the gut exhale the same smell of shit.

Of course, France wouldn't be the country of world citizenism (no doubt in a not-too-distant future *Le Monde Diplomatique* will be translated into more languages than *Capital*), the ridiculous epicenter of phobic opposition that claims to challenge the Market in the name of the *State*, had THEY not managed to make themselves so utterly impervious to all that is politically actual, and particularly impervious to 1970s Italy. From Paris to Porto Alegre, in country after country, the global expansion of ATTAC bears witness to this Bloomesque craze for quitting the world.

> *'77 wasn't like '68. '68 was anti-establishment, '77*
> *was radically alternative. This is why the "official"*
> *version portrays '68 as good and '77 as bad; in fact,*
> *'68 was co-opted whereas '77 was annihilated. This is*
> *why, unlike '68, '77 could never make for an easy*
> *object of celebration.*

— Nanni Balestrini, Primo Moroni, *L'orda d'oro*

On several occasions over the course of the 1970s the insurrectionary situation in Italy threatened to spread to France. It would last more than ten years and THEY would finally put an end to it with the arrest of more than 4,000 people. First, there were the wildcat strikes during the "Hot Autumn" (1969), which Empire quashed in the Piazza Fontana bombing massacre. The French, whose "working class took up the red flag of proletarian revolution from the students' delicate hands" only in order to sign the Grenelle Accords, couldn't believe that a movement originating in the universities could reach all the way to the factories. With all the bitterness of their abstract relationship with the working class, they felt deeply offended because their May came out sullied as a result. So they called the Italian situation "creeping May."

Ten years later, at a time when we were already happy to celebrate the *memory* of the French May, and at a time when its most resolute actors had already quietly found jobs within Republican institutions, new rumblings again came from Italy. These were more obscure, both because pacified French minds were already at a loss to understand much about a war in which they had, nevertheless, been engaged and because contradictory rumors sometimes mentioned prison revolts, sometimes an armed counterculture, sometimes the Red Brigades (BR), among all the other things that were a bit too *physical* for THEM to understand in France. We pricked up our ears, just out of curiosity, then we turned back to our petty concerns, telling ourselves that those Italians sure were naïve to continue the revolt when we had already moved on to commemoration.

THEY settled back into denunciations of the gulag, the "crimes of communism," and other delights of the "New Philosophy." THEY thereby avoided seeing that the Italians were revolting *against what May '68 had become, for example, in France.* Grasping that the movement in Italy "challenged the profs who gloried in their May-'68 past, because they were in reality the most fervent champions of social-democratic standardization" (*Tutto Città 77*)—that surely would have given the French an unpleasant taste of immediate history. Honor intact, THEY therefore became all the more certain of a "creeping May," thanks to which THEY could pack away the Movement of '77 with the souvenirs of another age, a movement from which everything is no less still to come.

Kojève, who was unmatched in cutting to the heart of the matter, offered a nice turn of phrase to put the French May to rest. During a meeting at the OECD a few days before he died of a heart attack, he observed of the "events": "There were no deaths. Nothing happened." Naturally, a bit more was needed to inter Italy's creeping May. Then another Hegelian surfaced who had acquired no less a reputation than the first but through different means. He said: "Listen, listen, nothing happened in Italy. Just some dead-enders manipulated by the state who wanted to terrorize the population by kidnapping some politicians and killing some judges. As you can see for yourselves, nothing exceptional." In this way, thanks to Guy Debord's shrewd intervention, on this side of the Alps we have never known that something happened in Italy in the 1970s. To this day, French luminaries have accordingly confined themselves to platonic speculations concerning the manipulation of the BR by this or that state service and the Piazza Fontana massacre. If Debord was an execrable middleman for all that was explosive in the Italian situation, he nonetheless introduced France to the favorite sport of Italian journalism: *retrology*. For the

Italians, retrology—a discipline whose first axiom might be "the truth is elsewhere"—refers to this paranoid game of mirrors played by those who no longer believe in any event, in any vital phenomenon, and who, consequently, that is, *as a consequence of their illness*, must always imagine someone or some group hidden behind what happens—the P2 Lodge, the CIA, Mossad, or even they themselves. The winner is the one who has given his little playmates the best reasons to doubt reality.

It is thus easier to understand why the French speak of a "creeping May" when it comes to Italy. They have the proud, public May, the state May.

In Paris May 68 has served as the *symbol* of '60s and '70s world political antagonism to the exact extent that the *reality* of this antagonism lies elsewhere.

No effort was spared, however, in transmitting to the French a bit of the Italian insurrection; there were *A Thousand Plateaus* and *Molecular Revolution*, there were Autonomy and the "squat" movement, but nothing had enough firepower to break through the wall of lies of the French spirit. Nothing that THEY can claim not to have foreseen. Instead, THEY prefer to chatter on about the Republic, Education, Social Security, Culture, Modernity and Social Relations, Suburban Unrest, Philosophy, and the Public Sector.

And this is still what THEY chatter on about just as the imperial services resurrect Italy's "strategy of tension." Clearly, there is an elephant missing from the glassworks. Someone to state the obvious, to come out with it somewhat coarsely and once and for all— even if it means smashing up the place a bit.

Here I would like to speak to the "comrades," among others, to those with whom I can share the party. I am a little fed up with the comfortable theoretical backwardness of the French ultra-left. I am fed up with hearing the same fake debates with their rhetorical sub-Marxism: spontaneity or organization, communism or anarchism, the human community or unruly individuality. There are still Bordigists, Maoists, and councilists in France. Not to mention the periodic Trotskyist revivals and Situationist folklore.

> *What was happening to the movement was clear: the union and the PCI came down on us like the police, like fascists. It was clear then that there was an irreparable divide between them and us. It was clear from then on that the PCI would no longer be entitled to speak within the movement.*
>
> — A witness to the clashes at the University of Rome on February 17, 1977, quoted in *L'Orda d'Oro*.

In his final book, Mario Tronti observes that "the workers' movement wasn't defeated by capitalism; the workers' movement was defeated by democracy." But democracy didn't defeat the workers' movement as if the workers' movement were a kind of foreign creature: it defeated it *as its internal limit*. The working class was only temporarily the privileged site of the proletariat, of the proletariat as "a class of civil society which is not a class of civil society," as "an estate that is the dissolution of all estates" (Marx).[9] Starting in the interwar period the proletariat began to definitively surpass the working class to the point that the most advanced segments of the Imaginary Party began to recognize in it, in its fundamental laborism, in its supposed "values," in its classist self-satisfaction, in short: in its class-being, the equivalent of the class-being of the bourgeoisie, its most formidable enemy and the most powerful vector for integration into the society of Capital. From then on the Imaginary Party would be the form in which the proletariat would appear.

In all Western countries '68 marks the meeting and collision of the old workers' movement—fundamentally socialist and senescent—with the first *constituted* segments of the Imaginary Party. When two bodies collide the direction that results depends on the inertia and mass of each. The same thing happened in every country. Where the workers' movement was still strong, as in Italy and France, the meager detachments of the Imaginary Party slipped into its moth-eaten forms, aping its language and methods. We then see the revival of militant practices of the "Third International" type; it ushered in groupuscular hysteria and neutralization via political abstraction. It was the short-lived triumph of Maoism and Trotskyism in France (the GP, PC-MLF, UJC-ML, JCR, Parti des Travailleurs, etc.),[10] of the *partitini* (Lotta continua, Avanguardia Operaia, MLS, Potere Operaio, Manifesto)[11] and other extra-parliamentary groups in Italy. Where the workers' movement had long been eliminated, as in the United States or Germany, there was an immediate move from student revolt to armed struggle, a move during which the use of the Imaginary Party's practices and tactics was often veiled in socialist or even Third-Worldist rhetoric. Hence, in Germany, the Movement 2 June, the Red Army Faction (RAF), the Rote Zellen, and in the United States, the Black Panther Party, the Weathermen, the Diggers or the Manson Family, were the emblems of a prodigious movement of internal defection.

The particularity of Italy in this context is that the Imaginary Party, although merged overwhelmingly with the socialist structures of the *partitini*, still found the strength to destroy them. Four years after '68 had revealed the "crisis of hegemony of the workers' movement" (R. Rossanda), the cauldron finally boiled over in 1973, leading to the first significant uprising of the Imaginary Party in a key area of Empire: the Movement of '77.

The workers' movement was beaten by democracy, that is, nothing to come out of this tradition can counter the new configuration of hostilities. On the contrary. When the hostis is no longer a portion of society—the bourgeoisie—but the society as such, the society as *power*, and when, therefore, we find ourselves fighting not against classical tyrannies but against biopolitical democracies, we know that every weapon, just like every strategy, must be reinvented. The hostis is Empire, and, for Empire, we are the Imaginary Party.

> *You're not from the castle,*
> *you're not from the village,*
> *you're nothing.*
> — Franz Kafka, *The Castle*[12]

The revolutionary element is the proletariat, the rabble. The proletariat is not a class. As the Germans of the nineteenth century still recognized, *es gibt Pöbel in allen Ständen*, there is a rabble in all classes. "Poverty in itself does not reduce people to a rabble; a rabble is created only by the disposition associated with poverty, by inward rebellion against the rich, against society, the government, etc. It also follows that those who are dependent on contingency become frivolous and lazy, like the *lazzaroni* of Naples, for example" (Hegel, *Elements of the Philosophy of Right*, addition to § 244).[13] Every time that it has attempted to define itself as a class, the proletariat has lost itself, taken the dominant class, the bourgeoisie, for a model. As a non-class, the proletariat is not the opposite of the bourgeoisie but of the *petite bourgeoisie*. Whereas the petty bourgeois believes himself capable of mastering the game of society, persuaded that he will come through all right individually, the proletariat knows that its fate hangs on its cooperating with its own kind, that it needs the latter in order to persist in being, in short: that its individual existence is fundamentally collective. In other words: *the proletariat is that which experiences itself as a form-of-life.* It is communist or nothing.

In every age the form in which the proletariat appears is redefined according to the overall configuration of hostilities. The most regrettable confusion in this regard concerns the "working class." As such, the working class has always been hostile to the revolutionary movement, to communism. It wasn't socialist by chance but socialist *in essence.* If we except the plebian elements, that is, specifically, what it was *unable* to recognize as *a worker*, the workers' movement has throughout its existence coincided with the *progressive* elements of capitalism. From February 1848 to the Commune and the autogestionary utopias of the 1970s, it has only ever demanded, for its most radical elements, the right of the working-class to *manage Capital for itself.* In reality, the proletariat has only ever worked for the expansion of the human basis of Capital. The so-called "socialist" regimes have carried out its program perfectly: integrating *everyone* into capitalist relations of production and incorporating *each person* into the process of valorization. Their collapse, conversely, has but shown the impossibility of a total capitalist system. It has thus been *by way of social* struggles and not against them that Capital has taken hold of humanity, that humanity has *in fact reappropriated it* to become, strictly speaking, *the people of Capital*. The workers' movement was therefore essentially a *social* movement, and it is as such that it has survived. In May 2001 a little tyrant from the Italian *Tute Bianche* came to explain to the young imbeciles of "Socialisme par en bas"[14] how to speak convincingly to power, how to sneak through the backdoor into the sticky game of classical politics. He explained the *Tute bianche* "approach" like this: "To us, the *Tute Bianche* symbolize all the subjects that have been absent from institutional politics, all those who aren't represented: illegal immigrants, young people, precarious workers, drug addicts, the homeless, the excluded. What we want is to give a voice to people who have none." Today's social movement, with its neo-trade-unionists, its informal activists, its spectacular spokesmen, its nebulous Stalinism, and its micro-politicians, is in this the heir of the workers' movement: it uses the inclusion of workers in the process of reformed valorization as a bargaining chip with the conservative agents of Capital. In exchange for doubtful institutional recognition—doubtful because of the logical impossibility of representing the unrepresentable, the proletariat—the workers' movement and then the social movement have promised Capital to maintain social peace. When, after Gothenburg, one of its sterile muses Susan George denounces the "rioters" whose methods "are as undemocratic as the institutions they mean to protest"; when in Genoa *Tute Bianche* deliver up to the cops supposed members of nonexistent "Black Blocs"—which they paradoxically decry as being infiltrated by the very same police—the representatives of the social movement have never failed to remind me of the reaction of the Italian workers' party when confronted with the Movement of '77. "The popular masses," reads the report Paolo Bufalini presented to the PCI Central Committee on April 18, 1978, "all citizens of democratic and civic feeling will continue their efforts to provide valuable assistance to the forces of order and to the officers and soldiers involved in the fight against terrorism. The priority is to isolate, both politically and morally, the red *brigatisti*, as well as their sympathizers and supporters, in order to strip them of any kind of alibi, of all external cooperation and support. They must be completely cut off and left like fish out of water, which is no small task when you consider how many people must be involved in these criminal activities." Because no one is more interested than the social movement in maintaining order, it was, is, and will be on the avant-garde of the war waged against the proletariat. From now on: against the Imaginary Party.

The history of Italy's creeping May demonstrates better than anything how the workers' movement has always been the vehicle for Capital-Utopia, a "community of work in which there are only producers, with no idle or homeless, and which would manage capital without crises and without inequality, capital having in this way become The Society" (Philippe Riviale, *La ballade du temps passé*).[15] Contrary to what the phrase suggests, creeping May was in no way a continuous process stretched out over ten years; it was rather an often cacophonous chorus of local revolutionary processes, moving, town by town, according to a distinctive rhythm marked by interruptions and resumptions, stases and accelerations, and each one reacting to the other. On common consensus a decisive rupture occurred, however, when the PCI adopted its politics of Historic Compromise in 1973. The preceding period, from 1968 to 1973, had been marked by the struggle between the PCI and extra-parliamentary groups for hegemony over the new social antagonisms. Elsewhere this had led to the success of the "second" or "new" left. The focus at the time was on what THEY called a "political solution," that is, the transformation of concrete struggles into alternative, more inclusive management of the capitalist state; struggles which the PCI at first considered favorably, and even encouraged here and there, since they helped enhance its contractual power. But starting in 1972 the new cycle of struggle began to run out of steam worldwide. It then became urgent for the PCI to cash in on a potential for social agitation whose price was in free fall. Moreover, the lesson of

Chili—where a socialist party whose rise to power in short order ended in a remote-controlled imperial putsch—tended to dissuade the PCI from going it alone in its bid for political hegemony. That was when the PCI laid out the terms for the Historic Compromise.

With the workers' party joining the party of order and the subsequent end of that sphere of representation, all political mediation disappeared. The Movement was isolated, forced to develop its own position from a non-class-based perspective; the extra-parliamentary groups and their phraseology was abruptly dropped; under the paradoxical effect of the watchword "des/agregazione" the Imaginary Party began to form a plane of consistency. At each new stage of the revolutionary process it logically came up against the most resolute of its adversaries, the PCI. Thus the most intense confrontations of the Movement of '77—whether in Bologna or at the University of Rome between Autonomists and the Metropolitan Indians on one side and the head of the CGIL's,[16] Luciano Lama's, stewards and the police on the other—would pit the Imaginary Party against the workers' party; and later on it was naturally the "red judges" who launched the "anti-terrorist" legal offensive and its series of police sweeps in 1979–1980. This is where one must look to find the origin of the "citizens" discourse currently promulgated in France as well as its offensive strategic function; this is the context in which it must be assessed. "It is utterly clear," wrote PCI members at the time, "that the terrorists and militants of subversion intend to thwart the workers' progressive march towards political leadership of the country, to attack the strategy of an expansion of democracy and the participation of the popular masses, to challenge the decisions of the working class in order to drag it into direct confrontation and, tragically, into ripping up the democratic fabric of society. [...] If large numbers mobilize in this country, if democratic forces intensify their unified action, if the government can give firm direction to state institutions that have been appropriately reformed and made more effective, terrorism and subversion will be isolated and vanquished and democracy will flourish in a thoroughly modernized state" (*Terrorisme et démocratie*). The call to denounce this or that person as a terrorist was thus the call to differentiate oneself from oneself *as capable of violence*, to project far from oneself one's latent warlike tendency, to introduce in oneself the economic disjunction that makes us a political subject, a citizen. It was therefore in still very relevant terms that Giorgio Amendola, then a PCI senior deputy, in due course attacked the Movement of '77: "Only those who seek the destruction of the republican state gain from spreading panic and preaching revolt." That's it exactly.

> *The points, knots, or focuses of resistance are spread over time and space at varying densities, at times mobilizing groups or individuals in a definitive way, inflaming certain points of the body, certain moments of life, certain types of behavior. Are there no great radical ruptures, massive binary divisions, then? Occasionally, yes. But more often one is dealing with mobile and transitory points of resistance, producing cleavages in a society that shift about, fracturing unities and effecting regroupings, furrowing across individuals themselves, cutting them up and remolding them, marking off irreducible regions in them, in their bodies and minds. Just as the network of power relations ends by forming a dense web that passes through apparatuses and institutions, without being exactly localized in them, so too the swarm of points of resistance traverses social stratifications and individual unities. And it is doubtless the strategic codification of these points of resistance that makes a revolution possible.*
> — Michel Foucault, *The History of Sexuality, Vol. 1* [17]

Empire is the kind of domination that knows no Outside, that has gone so far as to sacrifice itself as the Same in order to rid itself of the Other. Empire excludes nothing, substantially; it only precludes that anything present itself as *other*, that anything escape the general equivalence. The Imaginary Party is therefore nothing, specifically; it is everything that impedes, undermines, defies, ruins equivalence. Whether it speaks with the voice of a Putin, Bush, or Jiang Zemin, Empire will thus always label its hostis a "criminal," a "terrorist," a "monster." If need be, it will itself secretly organize "terrorist" and "monstrous" acts which it will then ascribe to the hostis—who remembers Boris Yeltsin's edifying rhetorical flights following the attacks in Moscow carried out by his own special police, especially his speech to the Russian people during which the buffoon called for a fight against Chechen terrorism, "against a domestic enemy that has no conscience, no pity, and no honor," that "has no face, no nationality, or religion"? On the other hand, Empire will never recognize its own military operations as acts of war, but only as "peace-keeping" operations, "international policing" efforts.

Before '68 brought the dialectic swaggering back— the dialectic *as the way of thinking final reintegration*— Marcuse attempted to think through this curious configuration of conflict. In a speech from 1966 entitled "The Concept of Negation in the Dialectic," Marcuse attacks the Hegelo-Marxist propensity to introduce negation *within* an antagonistic whole, whether between two classes, between the socialist camp and the capitalist camp, or between Capital and labor. To this tendency he opposes a contradiction,

*where does
negation come
from*

a negation that comes *from outside*. He observes that
the staging of social conflict *within* a totality, which
had been the defining characteristic of the workers'
movement, is but the mechanism by which THEY
freeze out the event, prevent the actual negation from
occurring *from the outside*. "The outside about which
I have spoken is not to be understood mechanistically
in the spatial sense but, on the contrary, as the
qualitative difference which overcomes the existing
antitheses inside the antagonistic partial whole [...]
and which is not reducible to these antitheses. [...]
[T]he force of negation is concentrated in no one
class. Politically and morally, rationally and instinc-
tively, it is a chaotic, anarchistic opposition: the refusal
to join and play a part, the disgust at all prosperity, the
compulsion to protest. It is a feeble, unorganized
opposition which nonetheless rests on motives and
purposes which stand in irreconcilable contradiction
to the existing whole."[18]

The new configuration of conflict came out of the
interwar period. On the one hand, there was Soviet
membership in the League of Nations, the Franco-
Soviet Pact, the failed strategy of the Comintern, the
masses joining with Nazism, fascism, and Francoism;
in short: the workers' betrayal of their call to revolution. On the other hand, there was the explosion of
social subversion coming from outside the workers'
movement—from surrealism, Spanish anarchism, or

the American hobos. Suddenly, the revolutionary movement and the workers' movement were no longer identical, revealing the Imaginary Party as an *excess* relative to the latter. The motto, "class against class," which from 1926 had become hegemonic, only reveals its latent content if we note that it predominated exactly at the moment when all classes began to disintegrate under the effect of the crisis. "Class against class" actually means "classes against the non-class"; it belies the determination to reabsorb, to liquidate this evermore massive *remainder*, this floating, socially unaccountable element that threatens to undermine every substantialist interpretation of society, be it bourgeois or Marxist. *Indeed, Stalinism must first of all be interpreted as the hardening of the workers' movement as it is effectively surpassed by the Imaginary Party.*

One group, the Cercle Communiste Démocratique, which united around [Boris] Souvarine in France in the 1930s, tried to redefine historical conflict. It succeeded by half in so far as it identified the two principal pitfalls of Marxism: economism and eschatology. The last issue of its revue *La Critique Sociale* noted the following failure: "Neither the liberal bourgeoisie nor the unconscious proletariat have shown themselves able to absorb into their political organizations the forces of the young and déclassé elements, whose increasingly energetic

interventions have accelerated the course of events"
(*La Critique Sociale*, no. 11, March 1934). As is hardly
surprising in a country where the custom is to dilute
everything—especially politics—in literature, the
first rough theory of the Imaginary Party comes from
the pen of Bataille in the revue's last issue. The article
is entitled "The Psychological Structure of Fascism."
For Bataille, the Imaginary Party stands in opposition
to *homogeneous society.* "Production is the basis of
social *homogeneity. Homogeneous* society is productive
society, namely, useful society. Every useless element
is excluded, not from all of society, but from its
homogeneous part. In this part, each element must be
useful to another without the homogeneous activity
ever being able to attain the form of activity *valid in
itself.* A useful activity has a common measure with
another useful activity, but not with activity *for itself.*
The common measure, the foundation of social
homogeneity and of the activity arising from it, is
money, namely the calculable equivalent of the different products of collective activity." Bataille here
points to the present-day composition of the world
into *a continuous biopolitical fabric,* which alone
accounts for the fundamental solidarity between
democratic and totalitarian regimes, for their infinite
reciprocal reversibility. The Imaginary Party is what
consequently manifests itself as *heterogeneous* to
biopolitical formation. "The very term *heterogeneous*
indicates that it concerns elements which are impossible

to assimilate; this impossibility which has a fundamental impact on social assimilation, likewise has an
impact on scientific assimilation. [...] *Violence, excess,
delirium, madness* characterize heterogeneous elements
to varying degrees: active, as persons or mobs, they
result from breaking the laws of social *homogeneity.*
[...] In summary, compared to everyday life, *heterogeneous* existence can be represented as *something
other*, as *incommensurate*, by charging these words
with the *positive* value they have in affective experience. [...] This proletariat cannot actually be limited
to itself: it is in fact only a point of concentration for
every dissociated social element that has been banished
to heterogeneity."[19] Bataille's error, which would
plague all the work of the College of Sociology and
Acéphale, was to continue to conceive of the
Imaginary Party *as a part of society*, to consider society
as a cosmos, as a whole capable of being represented
as beyond oneself, and to view oneself from this
perspective, i.e., from the point of view *of representation*.
All the ambiguity of Bataille's positions with regard
to fascism stems from his attachment to these used-up
dialectics, to all that prevented him from understanding that under Empire *the negation comes from
the outside*, that it does not occur as a heterogeneity
with respect to the homogeneous, but as a heterogeneity
in itself, as a heterogeneity *between* forms-of-life
playing within their difference. In other words, the
Imaginary Party can never be individuated as a

subject, a body, a thing, or a substance, nor even as a set of subjects, bodies, things, and substances, but only as the *event* of all of these things. The Imaginary Party is not substantially a remainder of the social whole, but the *fact* of this remainder, the fact that *there is a remainder*, that the represented always exceeds its representation, that over which power is exercised always eludes it. Here lies the dialectic— our condolences.

There is no "revolutionary identity." Under Empire, it is instead non-identity, the fact of constantly betraying the predicates that THEY hang on us, that is revolutionary. For a long time now, there have only been "revolutionary subjects" *for power*. To become neither particular nor general [*quelconque*], to become imperceptible, to conspire, means to distinguish between our presence and what we are for representation, in order to play with representation. To the exact extent that Empire becomes unified, that the new configuration of conflict acquires an objective character, there is a strategic necessity to know what we are for Empire, although accepting ourselves as such, as a "Black Bloc," an "Imaginary Party," or something else, would be the end of us. *For Empire, the Imaginary Party is but the form of pure singularity*. From the point of view of representation, singularity as such is the complete abstraction, the empty identity of the here and now. Likewise, from the point of view of the homogeneous, the Imaginary Party is simply "the heterogeneous," the purely unrepresentable. If we don't want to do the police's work for them, we will therefore have to be careful not to think we can do any more than *indicate the Imaginary Party when it occurs*—for instance: describe it, identify it, localize it within the territory or mark it out as a segment of "the society." The Imaginary Party is not one of the terms of social contradiction but *the fact that contradiction exists at all,* the inassimilable alterity of the determined faced with the omnivorous universality of Empire. And it is only for Empire, *that is, for representation*, that the Imaginary Party exists as such, that is, *as negative*. Dressing up what is hostile to the system of representation in the guise of the "negative," "protest," the "rebel," is simply a tactic that the system uses to bring within its plane of inconsistency the positivity it lacks—even at the risk of confrontation. The cardinal error of all subversion therefore lies in the obsession with negativity, in an attachment to the power of negation as if that were its most characteristic feature, whereas it is precisely in the power of negation that subversion is the most dependent on Empire, and on Empire's recognition of it. Here militancy like militarism finds its only desirable solution: that of ignoring our positivity, which is our whole strength, which is all that we have to offer, from the point of view of representation, that is, as derisory. And, of course, for Empire, *every determination is a negation.*

Foucault, too, made a decisive contribution to the theory of the Imaginary Party: his interviews dealing with the plebs. Foucault evokes the theme for the first time in a "Discussion with Maoists" on "popular justice" in 1972. Criticizing the Maoist practice of popular courts, he reminds us that all popular revolts since the Middles Ages have been *anti-judicial,* that the constitution of people's courts during the French Revolution occurred at precisely the moment when the bourgeoisie regained control, and, finally, that the tribunal form, by reintroducing a *neutral* authority between the people and its enemies, reincorporated the principle of the state in the struggle against the state. "When we talk about courts we're talking about a place where the struggle between contending forces is willy-nilly suspended."[20] According to Foucault, the function of justice following the Middles Ages was to separate the proletarianized plebs—the plebs integrated as a proletariat, included by way of their exclusion—from the non-proletarianized plebs, from the plebs proper. By isolating within the mass of the poor the "criminals," the "violent," the "insane," the "vagrants," the "perverted," the "gangsters," the "underworld," THEY would not only remove what was for power the most dangerous segment of the population, that which was always ready for armed, insurrectionary action, THEY would also enable themselves to turn the people's most offensive elements against the people themselves. This would be the permanent threat of "either you go to prison or you join the army," "either you go to prison or you leave for the colonies," "either you go to prison or you join the police," etc. All the effort of the workers' movement to distinguish between honest, strike-ready workers from "agitators," "rioters," and other "uncontrollable elements" is an extension of this opposition between the plebs and the proletariat. The same logic is at work today when gangsters become security guards: in order to neutralize the Imaginary Party by playing one of its parts off the others.

Foucault would clarify the notion of the plebs four years later in another interview. "No doubt it would be mistaken to conceive the 'plebs' as the permanent ground of history, the final objective of all subjections, the ever smoldering center of all revolts. The 'plebs' no doubt has no sociological reality. But there is indeed always something, in the social body, in classes, in groups, in individuals themselves, that in some way escapes power relations, something that is by no means the more or less docile or recalcitrant raw material, but rather the centrifugal movement, the inverse energy, the breakaway part. No doubt 'the' plebs does not exist, but there is, as it were, a certain plebeian quality or aspect ('de la' plèbe). There is plebs in bodies, in souls, in individuals, in the proletariat, in the bourgeoisie, but with an extension of forms, of energies, of various irreducibilities. This part of plebs is less exterior to power relations than their limit, their underside, their counterstroke, that which responds to every advance of power with a movement of disengagement. Hence it provides the motivation for every new development of networks of power. [...] This point of view of the plebs, the point of view of the underside and limit of power, is thus indispensable for an analysis of its apparatuses."[21]

But we owe the most decisive contribution to the theory of the Imaginary Party neither to a French writer nor to a French philosopher but rather to the militants of the Red Brigades Renato Curcio and Alberto Franceschini. In 1982, in a supplement to *Corrispondenza internazionale*, the little volume *Gocce di sole nelle città degli spettri* [Drops of sun in the city of specters] was published. As disagreements between Moretti's Red Brigades and their then-imprisoned "historical bosses" turned to open war, Curcio and Franceschini drew up the program of the short-lived Guerrilla Party, the third offshoot of the BR to form following its implosion, alongside the Walter Alasia Column and the BR-Combatant Communist Party. In the wake of the Movement of '77, remarking how much they were *spoken about* in the conventional Third International rhetoric of the revolution, they broke with the classical paradigm of production, taking the latter out of the factory and extending it to the Total Factory of the metropolis where semiotic production, that is, a *linguistic* paradigm of production, prevailed. "Rethought as a totalizing system (differentiated into private, interdependent, functional subsystems or fields of autonomous decision-making and auto-regulating capacity), that is, as a modular-corporate system, the computerized metropolis appears as a vast, barely disguised penal colony, in which each social system, just as each individual moves in passageways strictly differentiated and regulated by the whole. A penal colony made transparent by the computer networks that keep it under constant surveillance. In this model, metropolitan social space-time mimics the schema of a predictable universe in precarious equilibrium, unbothered by its forced tranquility, subdivided into modular compartments inside of which each worker labors, encapsulated within a specific collective role—like a goldfish in a bowl. A universe regulated by apparatuses of selective retroaction dedicated to the neutralization of all disruptions to the programs system established by the executive. [...] Given the absurd and unsustainable communication in which everyone is inevitably caught, as if ensnared by the paradoxical injunction—that in order to 'speak' one must give up 'communicating,' that to 'communicate' one must give up speaking!—

it isn't surprising that antagonistic communication strategies emerge which refuse the authorized language of power; it isn't surprising that the significations produced through domination are rejected and countered with new decentralized productions. Unauthorized, illegitimate productions, but organically connected to life, and which consequently constellate and constitute the secret *underground* network of resistance and self-defense against the computerized aggression of the insane idioms of the state. [...] Therein lies the main barrier separating social revolution from its enemies: the former takes in isolated resisters and schizo-metropolitan flows to a communicational territory antagonistic to that which led to their devastation and revolt. [...] In the ideology of control, an at-risk dividual is already synonymous with a 'potential terrorist madman,' with a fragment of high-explosive social material. That is why these dividuals are tracked down, spied on, and followed with the discretion and tireless rigor of the hunter by the great eye and the great ear. For the same reason they are made the target of an intense, intimidating semiotic bombardment that sustains the scraps of official ideology. [...] This is how the metropolis achieves its specificity as a concentration camp which, in order to deflect the incessant social antagonism it generates, simultaneously integrates and manipulates the artifices of seduction and fantasies of fear. Artifices and fantasies that assume the central function of the nervous system of the dominant culture and reconfigure the metropolis into an immense psychiatric *Lager—the most total of total institutions*—a labyrinthine network of High Security Quarters, areas of continuous control, loony bins, prisoner containers, reserves for volunteer metropolitan slaves, bunkered zones for demented fetishes. [...] In the metropolis, perpetrating violence against the necrotropic fetishes of Capital is humanity's greatest possible conscious act because it is through this social practice that the proletariat constructs—by appropriating the vital productive process—its knowledge and its memory, that is, its social power. [...] Destroying the old world through revolutionary transgression and bringing forth from this destruction the surprising and multiple constellations of new social relations are simultaneous processes that are nonetheless of two distinct kinds. [...] Those responsible for creating the imaginary world prohibit themselves from communicating real life, turning real life into madness; they fabricate angels of seduction and little monsters of fear in order to display them to the miserable rabble through the networks and circuits that transmit the sanctioned hallucination. [...] To rise up from the 'registered location,' to take to the stage to wreck the fetishistic performance: that is what the metropolitan guerrillas of new communication have set out to do from the start. [...] Within the complex metropolitan revolutionary process, the party cannot have an exclusively or emi-nently political form. [...] Nor can the party take on an exclusively combative form. The 'power of arms' does not imply, as the militarists believe, absolute power, because absolute power is the power-knowledge that reunifies social practices. [...] A guerrilla party means: the party of power/party of knowledge. [...] The guerrilla party is the agent through which proletarian knowledge-power achieves its maximum exterioriza-tion and invisibility. [...] This means that the greater the party's invisibility, the more it opposes global imperialist counterrevolution, the greater its visibility, the more it becomes an internal part of the proletariat, that is to say, the more it communicates with the pro-letariat. [...] In this way, the guerrilla party is the party of transgressive social communication."

> *In large part it was these tendencies and not the violence of the struggles that made the young people of '77 incomprehensible to the traditional elements of the workers' movement.*
> — Paolo Virno, "Do You Remember Counter-revolution"[22]

Genoa is sacked by masked-bodied reayas, a new squat opens, workers threaten to blow up their factory, a suburb explodes, its inhabitants attack police stations and the nearest lines of communication, the end of a protest turns nasty, a field of transgenic corn is mowed down during the night. Whatever discourse describes these acts—Marxist-Leninist, reformist, Islamist, anarchist, socialist, ecologist, or stupidly critical—they are events of the Imaginary Party. It matters little if the discourses are fit from the first capital letter to the last period to the mould of meaning of Western metaphysics, for from the start these acts speak *a different language.*

For us, the aim is of course to combine with the event as gesture the event as language. This is what Autonomia Operaia achieved in Italy in the 1970s. Autonomia was never *one* movement, even if THEY

described it at the time as "the Movement." Autonomia's space was the plane of consistency where a large number of singular destinies flowed together, intersected, aggregated, and dis/aggregated. Bringing these destinies together under the term "Autonomia" serves purely as a signifying device, a misleading convention. The big misunderstanding here is that autonomy wasn't the predicate demanded by subjects—what dreary, democratic drivel if the whole thing had been about demanding one's autonomy as a subject—*but by becomings [devenirs]*. Autonomia thus has innumerable birthdates, is but a succession of opening acts, like so many *acts of secession*. It is, therefore, workers' autonomy, the autonomy of the unions' *rank and file*, of the rank and file that ransacked the headquarters of a moderate union at Piazza Statuto in Turin in 1962. But it is also workers' autonomy with regard to their *role* as workers: the refusal to work, sabotage, wildcat strikes, absenteeism, their declared estrangement from the conditions of their exploitation, from the capitalist whole. It is women's autonomy: the refusal of domestic work, the refusal to silently and submissively reproduce the masculine workforce, self-consciousness, making themselves heard, putting an end to pointless affective intercourse; women's autonomy, therefore, from their *role* as women and from patriarchal civilization. It is the autonomy of young people, of the unemployed, of the marginal, who refuse their role as outcasts, who are no longer willing to keep their mouths shut, who impose themselves on the political scene, demand a guaranteed income, create an armed struggle in order to be paid to sit on their asses. But it is also the autonomy of militants from the *figure* of the militant, from the *partinini*, and from the logic of the groupuscule, from a conception of action always deferred—deferred until later in existence. Contrary to what the sociologizing half-wits—always hungry for profitable reductions—may lead one to believe, the remarkable fact here is not the affirmation of "new subjects," whether political, social, or productive, young people, women, the unemployed, or homosexuals, but rather their violent, practical, active desubjectivation, the rejection and betrayal of the role that has been assigned to them *as subjects.* What the different becomings of Autonomia have in common is their call for a *movement of separation* from society, from the whole. This secession is not the assertion of a static difference, of an essential alterity, a new entry on the balance sheet of identities managed by Empire, but a *flight*, a line of flight. At the time, separation was written *Separ/azione.*

The movement of internal desertion, of brutal subtraction, of ever-renewed flight, this chronic irreducibility to the world of domination—this is what Empire fears. "The only way to develop our culture and to live our lives, as far as we are concerned, is by being absent," proclaimed the Maoist-Dadaist fanzine *Zut* in its October '76 issue. That we could become absent to its provocations, indifferent to its values, that we might not respond to its stimuli—that is the permanent nightmare of cybernetic domination, "to which power responds by criminalizing all foreign behavior and one's rejection of capital" (*Vogliamo Tutto* 10, summer '76). Autonomy therefore means: desertion, deserting family, deserting the office, deserting school, deserting all supervision, deserting men's, women's, and the citizen's roles, deserting all the shitty relations in which THEY believe us to be held—endless desertion. With every new direction that we give to our movement, the essential thing is to increase our power [*puissance*], to always follow the line of increasing power in order to strengthen the force of our deterritorialization, to make sure that THEY won't be stopping us anytime soon. In all this, what we have most to fear, what we have most to *betray*, is all those who are watching us, who are tracking us, following us from afar, thinking of one way or another to capitalize the energy expended by our flight: all the managers, all the maniacs of reterritorialization. Some are on the side of Empire, of course: the trend-setters feeding on the cadaver of our inventions, the hip capitalists, and other dismal scum. But some can also be found on our side. In 1970s Italy they were the Operaists, the great unifiers of Autonomia Organizzata, which succeeded in "bureaucratizing the concept of 'autonomy' itself" (*Neg/azione*, 1976). They will always try to make ONE movement out of our movements in order to speak in its name, indulging in their favorite game: political ventriloquism. In the 1960s and 1970s the Operaists thus spent all their time repatriating in the terms and behavior of the workers' movement what in fact outstripped them on all sides. Taking as their starting point the ethical estrangement from work expressing itself overwhelmingly among workers recently emigrated from southern Italy, they theorized *workers' autonomy*—against the unions and the bureaucrats of the classical workers' movement—whose spontaneous meta-bureaucrats they were hoping to become; and this, without having to climb the hierarchical ladder of a classical union: a meta-syndicalism. Hence the treatment they reserved for the plebian elements of the working class, their refusal to allow the workers to become *something other* than workers, their obliviousness to the fact that the autonomy asserting itself wasn't *workers'* autonomy but autonomy *from* the worker identity. They subsequently treated "women," "the unemployed," "young people," "the marginal," in short, "the autonomous," all in the same way. Incapable of any familiarity with themselves let alone with any world, they desperately sought to transform a plane of consistency, the space of Autonomia, into an organization—a combatant organization, if possible—that would make them the last-chance interlocutors of a moribund power. Naturally, we owe the most remarkable and most popular travesty of the Movement of '77 to an Operaist theoretician, Asor Rosa: the so-called "theory of two societies." According to him, we were supposed to have witnessed a clash between two societies, that of workers with job security, on the one hand, and, on the other, that of workers without (young people, precarious workers, the unemployed, the marginal, etc.). Even if the theory has the virtue of breaking with the very thing that every socialism and, therefore, every left look to preserve (even if it takes a massacre to do it), namely, the fiction of society's ultimate unity, it neglects (1) that the "first society" no longer exists, having already begun a process of continuous implosion; (2) that the Imaginary Party, which is being constructed as the ethical fabric following the implosion, is in no way *one*, in any case, in no way capable of being unified into a new isolable whole: a second society. This is exactly the move that Negri now atavistically reproduces when he calls a singular *multitude* something whose essence is, in his own words, a multiplicity. The theoretical con game will never be as pathetic as its underlying goal, which is to pass oneself off as the organic intellectual of a new *spectacularly* unified subject.

For the Operaists *autonomy* was, therefore, part and parcel an autonomy of class, an autonomy of *a new social subject*. Over the twenty years of Operaist activity this axiom was maintained thanks to the convenient notion of *class composition*. As circumstances and short-sighted political calculations dictated, this or that new sociological category would be included in "class composition," and, on the pretext of a study of labor, one would reasonably change sides. When the workers got tired of fighting, the death of the "mass-worker" would be decreed and his role of global insurgent would be replaced with that of the "social worker," that is, with more or less anyone. Eventually we would end up discovering revolutionary virtues at Benetton, in the little Berlusconian entrepreneurs of the Italian North-East (cf. *Des entreprises pas comme les autres*)[23] and even, if need be, in the Northern League.

Throughout "creeping" May autonomy was nothing more than this incoercible movement of flight, this staccato of ruptures, in particular ruptures with the workers' movement. Even Negri acknowledges as much: "The bitter polemic that opened in '68 between the revolutionary movement and the official workers' movement turned into an irreversible rupture in '77," he says in *L'Orda d'Oro*.[24] Operaism, the outmoded *because avant-garde* consciousness of the Movement, would never tire of reappropriating this rupture, of interpreting it in terms of the workers' movement. In Operaism, just like in the practices of the BR, we find less an attack on capitalism than a covetous struggle with the leadership of the most powerful communist party in the West, the PCI, a struggle whose prize was power OVER the workers. "We could only talk politics by way of Leninism. As long as a different class composition wasn't in the offing, we found ourselves in a situation that many innovators have found themselves in: that of having to explain the new with an old language," Negri complains in an interview from 1980. It was therefore under cover of orthodox Marxism, under the protection of a rhetorical fidelity to the workers' movement, that the *false consciousness* of the movement came of age. There were voices, like those of *Gatti Selvaggi*, that spoke out against this sleight of hand: "We are against the 'myth' of the working class because it is first of all harmful to the working class. Operaism and populism only serve the millennial aim of using the 'masses' as a pawn in the dirty games of power" (no. 1, December 1974). But the fraud was too flagrant not to work. And, in fact, it worked.

Given the fundamental provincialism of French opposition movements, what happened thirty years ago in Italy isn't just historical anecdote; on the contrary: *we still haven't addressed* the problems the Italian autonomists faced at the time. Given the circumstances, the move from struggles over places of work to struggles over territory; the recomposition of the ethical fabric on the basis of secession; the reappropriation of the means to live, to struggle, and to communicate among ourselves form a horizon that remains unreachable as long as the existential prerequisite of separ/azione goes unacknowledged. Separ/azione means: we have nothing to do with this world. We have nothing to say to it nor anything to make it understand. Our acts of destruction, of sabotage: we have no reason to follow them up with an explanation duly guided by human Reason. We are not working for a better, alternative world to come, but in virtue of what we have already confirmed through experimentation, in virtue of the radical irreconcilability between Empire and this experimentation, of which war is a part. And when, in response to this massive critique, reasonable people, legislators, technocrats, those in power ask, "But what do you really want?" our response is, "We aren't citizens. We will never adopt your point of view of the whole, your *management* point of view. We refuse to play the game, that is it. It is not our job to tell you which sauce to cook us with." The main source of the paralysis from which we must break free is the utopia of the human community, the perspective of a final, universal reconciliation. Even Negri, at the time of *Domination and Sabotage*, took this step, the step outside socialism: "I don't see the history of class consciousness as Lukács does, as a fated, integral recomposition, but rather as a moment of intensively implanting myself in my own separation. I am *other*, other is the movement of collective praxis of which I am a part. I participate in *an other workers' movement*. Of course I know how much criticism speaking this way may provoke from the point of view of the Marxist tradition. I have the impression, as far as I am concerned, of holding myself at the extreme signifying limit of a political discourse on class. [...] I therefore have to accept radical difference as the methodical condition of subversion, of the project of proletarian self-valorization. And my relationship with the historical totality? With the totality of the system? Here we get to the second consequence of the assertion: my *relationship with the totality* of capitalist development, with the totality of historical development, is secure only through the *force of destructuration* determined by the movement, through the total *sabotage* of the history of capital undertaken by the movement. [...] I define myself by separating myself from the totality, and I define the totality as other than myself, as a network extending over the continuity of historical sabotage undertaken by the class. Naturally, there is no more an "other workers' movement" than there is a "second society." On the other hand, there are the incisive becomings of the Imaginary Party, and their autonomy.

*The most yielding thing in the world will overcome the
most rigid.*
— Lao Tzu, *Tao Te Ching*[25]

The first campaign against Empire failed. The RAF's
attack on the "imperialist system," the BR's on the SIM
(Stato Imperialista delle Multinazionali), and so many
other guerrilla groups have been easily suppressed. The
failure was not one of this or that militant organization, of this or that "revolutionary subject," but the
failure of *a conception of war*, of a conception of war
that could not be reproduced beyond the sphere of
organizations *because it itself was already a reproduction.*
With the exception of certain RAF texts or the
Movement 2 June, most documents from the
"armed struggle" are written in this ossified, used-
up, borrowed language that one way or another smells
of Third International kitsch. As if the point was to
dissuade anyone from joining.

After twenty years of counterrevolution, the second act
in the anti-imperialist struggle has now begun. Until
now, the collapse of the socialist bloc and the social-
democratic conversion of the last remnants of the
workers' movement have definitively freed our party

from any of the socialist inclinations it still may have had. Indeed, the obsolescence of the old conceptions of struggle first became obvious with the disappearance of the struggle itself, then with the "anti-globalization movement" of today, with the higher-order parody of former militant practices.

The return of war requires a new conception of warfare. *We must invent a form of war such that the defeat of Empire no longer obliges suicide, but rather to recognize ourselves as living, as more and more ALIVE.*

Our starting point is not fundamentally different from that of the RAF when it observes: "the system has taken up all of the free time people had. To their physical exploitation in the factory is now added the exploitation of their feelings and thoughts, wishes, and utopian dreams [...] through mass consumption and the mass media. [...] The system has managed, in the metropolises, to drag the masses so far down into its own dirt that they seem to have largely lost any sense of the oppressive and exploitative nature of their situation [...]. So that for a car, a pair of jeans, life insurance, and a loan, they will easily accept any outrage on the part of the system. In fact, they can no longer imagine or wish for anything beyond a car, a vacation, and a tiled bathroom."[26] The unique thing about Empire is that it has expanded its colonization over the whole of existence and over all that exists. It is not only that

Capital has enlarged its human base, but it has also deepened the moorings of its jurisdiction. Better still, on the basis of a final disintegration of society and its subjects, Empire now intends to recreate an ethical fabric, of which the hipsters, with their modular neighborhoods, their modular media, codes, food, and ideas, are both the guinea pigs and the avant-garde. And this is why, from the East Village to Oberkampf by way of Prenzlauer Berg, the *hip* phenomenon has so quickly had such worldwide reach.

It is on this *total* terrain, the ethical terrain of forms-of-life, that the war against Empire is currently being played out. It is a war of annihilation. Contrary to the thinking of the BR, for whom the explicit purpose of the Moro kidnapping was the armed party's recognition by the state, Empire is not the enemy. Empire is no more than the *hostile environment* opposing us at every turn. We are engaged in a struggle over the recomposition of an ethical fabric. This recomposition can be seen throughout the territory, in the process of progressive hipification of formerly secessionist sites, in the uninterrupted extension of chains of apparatuses. Here the classical, abstract conception of war, one culminating in a total confrontation in which war would finally reunite with its essence, is obsolete. War can no longer be discounted as an isolable moment of our existence, a moment of decisive confrontation; from now on *our very existence, every aspect of it, is war.*

That means that the first movement of this war is *reappropriation.* Reappropriation of the means of living-and-struggling. Reappropriation, therefore, of space: the squat, the occupation or communization of private spaces. Reappropriation of the common: the constitution of autonomous languages, syntaxes, means of communication, of an autonomous culture—stripping the transmission of experience from the hands of the state. Reappropriation of violence: the communization of combat techniques, the formation of self-defense forces, arms. Finally, reappropriation of basic survival: the distribution of medical power-knowledge, of theft and expropriation techniques, the progressive organization of an autonomous supply network.

Empire is well-armed to fight the two types of secession it recognizes: secession "from above" through golden ghettos—the secession, for example, of global finance from the "real economy" or of the imperial hyperbourgeoisie from the rest of the biopolitical fabric—and secession "from below" through "no-go areas"—housing projects, inner cities, and shantytowns. Whenever one or the other threatens its meta-stable equilibrium, Empire need only play one against the other: the civilized modernity of the trendy against the retrograde barbarism of the poor, or the demands for social cohesion and equality against the inveterate egotism of the rich. "One aims to impart political coherence to a social and spatial entity in order to avoid all risk of secession by territories inhabited either by those excluded from the socio-economic network or by the winners of the global economic dynamic. [...] Avoiding all forms of secession means finding the means to reconcile the demands of the new social class and the demands of those excluded from the economic network whose spatial concentration is such that it induces deviant behavior." These are the theories peddled by the advisers of Empire—in this case, Cynthia Ghorra-Gobin in *Les États-Unis entre local et mondial.*[27] That said, Empire is powerless to prevent the exodus, the secession, we are working towards precisely because the latter's territory is not only physical, but *total*. Sharing a technique, the turn of a phrase, a certain configuration of space suffices to activate our plane of consistency. Therein lies our strength: in a secession that cannot be recorded on the maps of Empire, because it is a secession neither from above nor from below, but a secession *through the middle*.

What we are simply getting at here is the constitution of *war machines*. By war machines should be understood a certain coincidence between living and struggling, a coincidence that is never given without simultaneously requiring its construction. Because each time one of these terms ends up separated, however it happens, from the other, the war machine degenerates, derails. If the moment of living is unilateralized, it becomes a *ghetto*. Proofs of this are the grim quagmires of the "alternative," whose specific task is to market the Same in the guise of difference. Most occupied social centers in Germany, Italy, or Spain clearly show how simulated exteriority from Empire provides a precious tool in capitalist valorization. "The ghetto, the apologia of 'difference,' the privilege accorded to moral and introspective questions, the tendency to form a separate society that forgoes attacks on the capitalist machine, on the 'social factory'—couldn't all this be a result of the approximate and rhapsodic 'theories' of Valcarenghi [head of the countercultural publication *Re Nudo*][28] and company? And isn't it strange that they call us a 'subculture' just as all their flowery, nonviolent crap has started to be undermined?" The *Senza Tregua* autonomists were writing this already in 1976. On the other hand, if the moment of struggle is hypostatized, the war machine degenerates into an *army*. All militant formations, all terrible communities are war machines that have survived their own extinction in this petrified form. The introduction to the collection of Autonomia texts *Il diritto all'odio* [The Right to Hate] published in 1977 already pointed to this excess of the war machine with regard to its acts of war: "Tracing the chronology of this hybrid and, in many regards, contradictory subject that materialized in the *sphere* of Autonomia, I find myself reducing the movement to a sum of events whereas the reality of its becoming-war-machine asserted itself only in the transformation that the subject effectuated concentrically *around* each moment of effective confrontation."[29]

There is no war machine except in movement, even hindered, even imperceptible movement, in movement following its propensity for increasing power. Movement insures that the power struggles traversing it never settle into power relations. We can win our war, that is, our war will continue, increase our power, provided that the confrontation is always subordinated to our positivity: *never strike beyond one's positivity*, such is the vital principle of every war machine. Each space conquered from Empire, from its hostile environment, must correspond to our capacity to fill it, to configure it, to inhabit it. Nothing is worse than a victory one doesn't know what to do with. In essence, then, ours will be a silent war; it will be evasive, avoid direct confrontation, declare little. In so doing it will impose its own temporality. Just as we are identified we will give the notice to disperse, never allowing ourselves to be suppressed, already reuniting in some unsuspected place. The location makes no difference since every local attack is henceforth an attack against Empire—that is the only worthwhile lesson to come out from the Zapatista farce. The important thing is never to lose the initiative, never let a hostile temporality impose itself. And above all: never forget that our strike capacity is linked to how well-armed we are only by virtue of our constitutive positivity.

I steer clear of those who expect fate, dreams, a riot to provide them with a way to escape their weakness. They are too much like those who in the past relied on God to save their wasted lives.
— Georges Bataille[30]

It is commonly acknowledged that the Movement of '77 was defeated because it was incapable, notably during the Bologna conference, of relating in any significant way to its offensive strength, to its "violence." In Empire's fight against subversion, its entire strategy consists in isolating the most "violent"— "punks," the "out of control," the "autonomous," "terrorists," etc.—from the rest of the population— and every year this is again proven true. Contrary to the police view of the world, it must be said that there is in fact no *problem* with armed struggle: no consequential struggle has ever been waged without arms. There is no problem with armed struggle except for the state, which wants to conserve its monopoly over legitimate armed force. On the other hand, there is indeed the question of the *use* of arms. When in March '77 100,000 people protested in Rome, 10,000 of whom were armed and, at the end of daylong confrontations, not one policeman was hurt although a massacre would have been easy, we can better appreciate the difference between being armed and using arms. Being armed is part of the power struggle, the refusal to remain abjectly at the mercy of the police, a way of assuming our legitimate impunity. Now that that is cleared up, there remains the question of our relationship with violence, a relationship whose general lack of consideration impedes the progress of anti-imperial subversion.

Every war machine is by nature a society, a society without a state; but under Empire, given its obsidional status, another determination has to be added. It is a society of a particular kind: a *warrior* society. Although each existence is at its core essentially a war and each will know how to engage in confrontation when the time comes, a minority of beings must take war as the *exclusive* aim of their existence. These are *the warriors*. Henceforth the war machine will have to defend itself not only from hostile attacks, but also from the threat of the warrior minority breaking off from it, composing a caste, a dominant class, forming an embryonic state and, by turning the offensive resources at its disposal into the means of oppression, taking power. To us, establishing a central relationship with violence only means establishing a central relationship with the warrior minority. Interestingly, it was in a text from 1977, the last by Clastres, *The Sorrows of the Savage Warrior*, that such a relationship was sketched out for the first time. It was perhaps necessary that all the propaganda about classical virility had to fade before such an undertaking could be made.

Contrary to what THEY have told us, the warrior is not a figure of plenitude, and certainly not of virile plenitude. The warrior is a figure of amputation. The warrior is a being who feels he exists only through combat, through confrontation with the Other, a being who is unable to obtain for himself the feeling of existing. In the end, nothing is sadder than the sight of a form-of-life that, in every situation, expects hand-to-hand combat to remedy its absence from itself. But nothing is more moving, either; because this absence from self is not a simple lack, a lack of familiarity with oneself, but rather a positivity. The warrior is in fact driven by a desire, and perhaps one sole desire: the desire to disappear. The warrior no longer wants to be, but wants his disappearance to have a certain style. He wants to *humanize* his vocation for death. That is why he never really manages to mix with the rest of humankind: they are spontaneously wary of his movement toward Nothingness. In their admiration for the warrior can be measured the distance they impose between him and them. The warrior is thus condemned to be alone. This leaves him greatly dissatisfied, dissatisfied because he is unable to belong to any community other than the false community, the *terrible* community, of warriors who have only their solitude in common. Prestige, recognition, glory are less the prerogative of the warrior than the only form of relationship compatible with his solitude. His solitude is at once his salvation and his damnation.

The warrior is a figure of anxiety and devastation. Because he isn't *present*, is only for-death, his immanence has become miserable, and he knows it. He has never gotten used to the world, so he has no attachment to it; he awaits its end. But there is also a tenderness, even a gentleness about the warrior, which is this silence, this half-presence. If he isn't present, it is often because otherwise he would only drag those around him into the abyss. That is how the warrior loves: by preserving others from the death he has at heart. Instead of the company of others, he thus often prefers to be alone, and this more out of kindness than disgust. Or else he joins the grief-stricken pack of warriors who watch each other slide one by one towards death. Because such is their inclination.

In a sense, the society to which the warrior belongs cannot help but distrust him. It doesn't exclude him nor really include him; it excludes him through its inclusion and includes him through its exclusion. The ground of their mutual understanding is *recognition*. In according him prestige society keeps the warrior at a distance, attaching itself to him and by the same token condemning him. "For each exploit accomplished," writes Clastres, "the warrior and society render the same judgment: the warrior says, 'That's good, but I can do more, increase my glory.' Society says, 'That's good, but you should do more, obtain our recognition of a superior prestige.' In other words, as much by his own personality (glory above all else) as by his total dependence on the tribe (who else could confer glory?), the warrior finds himself, *volens nolens*, the prisoner of a logic that relentlessly makes him want to do a little more. Lacking this, society would quickly forget his past exploits and the glory they procured for him. The warrior only exists in war; he is devoted as such to action" and, therefore, in short order, to death. If the warrior is in this way dominated, alienated from society, "the existence in a given society of an organized group of 'professional' warriors tends to transform the *permanent state of war* (the general situation of the primitive society) into *actual permanent war* (the situation specific to warrior societies). Such a transformation, pushed to the limit, would bring about considerable sociological consequences since by affecting the very structure of society it would alter its undivided being. The power to decide on matters of war and peace (an absolutely essential power) would in effect no longer belong to society as such, but indeed to the brotherhood of warriors, which would place its private interest before the collective interest of society, making its particular point of view the general point of view of the tribe. [...] First a group seeking *prestige*, the warlike community would then transform itself into a *pressure* group in order to push society into accepting the intensification of war."[31]

The subversive counter-society *must*, we *must* recognize the prestige connected to the exploits of every warrior, of every combatant organization. We *must* admire the courage of any feat of arms, the technical perfection of this or that exploit, of a kidnapping, of an assassination, of every successful armed action. We *must* appreciate the audacity of this or that prison attack meant to liberate comrades. We must do all this specifically in order to protect ourselves from warriors, *in order to condemn them to death*. "Such is the defense mechanism that primitive society erects to ward off the risk that the warrior, as such, presents: the life of the undivided social body for the death of the warrior. Tribal law becomes clear here: primitive society is, in its being, a *society-for-war*; it is at the same time, and for the same reasons, a *society against the warrior*."[32] There will be no doubt of our grief.

The Italian Movement's relationship with its armed minority was marked by this same ambivalence throughout the 1970s. The fear was that the minority would break off into an autonomous military force. And that is exactly what the state, with its "strategy of tension," was aiming at. By artificially raising the military presence in the conflict, by criminalizing political protest, by forcing the members of militant organizations underground, it wanted to cut the minority off from the Movement and in so doing to make it as hated within the Movement as the state already was. The idea was to liquidate the Movement as a war machine by compelling it to take as its *exclusive* objective war with the state. The watchword of the PCI secretary general, Berlinguer, in 1978—"You are either with the Italian state or with the BR"— which above all meant "either with the Italian state or with the Brigadist state"—sums up the *apparatus* by which Empire crushed the Movement, and which it is now exhuming in order to prevent the return of anti-capitalist struggle.

"But how many of there are you? I mean…of us, the group."

"Who knows. One day there are two of us, the next twenty. And sometimes when we meet, there are a hundred thousand."

— Cesare Battisti, *L'ultimo sparo* [The Last Shot][33]

In 1970s Italy two subversive strategies coexisted: that of militant organizations and that of Autonomia. This is an oversimplification. It is obvious, for example, that in the sole case of the BR, one can distinguish between the "first BR," those of Curcio and Franceschini—who were "invisible to power, but present for the movement"; who were implanted in factories where they kept the loudmouth bosses quiet, kneecapped scabs, burned cars, kidnapped managers; who only wanted to be, in their words, "the highest point of the movement"—and those of Moretti, more distinctly Stalinist, who went completely, professionally, underground, and who, having become invisible to the movement as much as to themselves, launched an "attack on the heart of the state" on the abstract stage of classical politics and ended up just as cut off from any ethical reality. It would therefore be possible to argue that the most famous of the BR's actions, Moro's kidnapping, his incarceration in a "prison of the people," where he was judged by a "proletarian court," so perfectly imitated the procedures of the state not to be, already, the exploit of a degenerate militarized BR, which was no longer what it once was, no longer looked anything like the first BR. If we forget these potential subtleties, we see that there is a strategic axiom common to the BR, the RAF, the NAP, Prima Linea (PL), and, in fact, to all combatant organizations, and that is to oppose Empire *as a subject*, a collective, revolutionary subject. It entails not only *calling for* acts of war, but above all forcing its members to eventually go underground and in so doing to sever themselves from the ethical fabric of the Movement, from its life as a war machine. A former PL member, surrounded by calls for his surrender, offered some worthwhile observations: "During the Movement of '77, the BR understood nothing of what was happening. The ones who had been working as moles for years suddenly saw thousands of young people doing whatever they wanted. As for Prima Linea, the movement had had influence, but paradoxically nothing remained of it, whereas the BR recuperated the remnants when the movement died out. In fact, the armed groups never knew how to get in synch with the existing movements. They reproduced a kind of alternative mechanism, a kind of silent infiltration, and finally, a virulent critique. And when the movement disappeared, the disillusioned leaders were gathered up and launched into the heights of Italian politics. […] This was especially the case after Moro. Before, the organization was instead run with this somewhat irrational spirit of transgression of the Movement of '77. We weren't modern-day Don Juans, but the prevailing behavior was 'unauthorized.' Then little by little the influence of the BR changed. They had their grand, model romance, the passion between Renato Curcio and Margherita Cagol. […] With militarism—a certain conception of militarism—life itself is organized as it is in the army. The analogy with the military struck me; this formal camaraderie infused with reassuring optimism which feeds a certain kind of competitiveness: whoever told the best joke and kept the troops' spirits up the best won. With—just as in the army—the gradual elimination of the shy and depressed ones of the group. There is no place for them, because they are immediately considered a weight on the regiment's morale. It is a typical military deformity: seeking in the exuberant and noisy existence of a gang a form of security that substitutes for an inner life. So, unconsciously, you have to marginalize those who might weigh things down with perhaps a morose but no doubt more sincere mood, in any case, a mood that must be a lot closer to what the noisiest must deep down be feeling inside. With a cult of virility as the result" (*Libération*, October 13–14, 1980). If we leave aside the profound ill will behind these remarks, the account confirms two mechanisms specific to every political group that is constituted as a subject, as an entity separated from the plane of consistency on which it depends: (1) It takes on all the features of a terrible community. (2) It finds itself projected into the realm of representation, into the sphere of classical politics, which alone shares with it its same degree of separation and spectrality. The subject-subject confrontation with the state necessarily follows, as an abstract rivalry, as the staging of an *in vitro* civil war; and finally one ends up attributing to the enemy a heart it doesn't have. One attributes to the enemy precisely that substance which one is on the point of losing.

The other strategy, not of war but of diffuse guerilla warfare, is the defining characteristic of Autonomia. It alone is capable of bringing down Empire. This doesn't mean curling up into a compact subject in order to confront the state, but disseminating oneself in a multiplicity of foci, like so many *rifts* in the capitalist whole. Automonia was less a collection of radio stations, bands, weapons, celebrations, riots, and squats, than a certain intensity in the circulation of bodies between all these points. Thus Autonomia didn't exclude the existence of other organizations within it, even if they held ridiculous neo-Leninist pretentions: each organization found a place within the empty architecture through which—as circumstances evolved—the flows of the Movement passed. As soon as the Imaginary Party becomes a secessionist ethical fabric the very possibility of instrumentalizing the Movement by way of its organizations, and a fortiori the very possibility of its infiltration, vanishes: rather, the organizations themselves will inevitably be subsumed by the Movement as simple *points* on its plane of consistency. Unlike combatant organizations, Autonomia was based on indistinction, informality, a semi-secrecy appropriate to conspiratorial practice. War acts were anonymous, that is, signed with fake names, a different one each time, in any case, unattributable, soluble in the sea of Autonomia. They were like so many marks etched in the half-light, and as such forming a denser and more formidable offensive than the armed propaganda campaigns of combatant organizations. Every act signed itself, claimed responsibility for itself through its particular *how*, through its specific meaning in situation, allowing one instantly to discern the extreme-right attack, the state massacre of subversive activities. This strategy, although never articulated by Autonomia, is based on the sense that not only is there no longer a revolutionary subject, but that it is *the non-subject itself* that has become revolutionary, that is to say, effective against Empire. By instilling in the cybernetic machine this sort of permanent, daily, endemic conflict, Autonomia succeeded in making the machine ungovernable. Significantly, Empire's response to this *any enemy* [*ennemi quelconque*] will always be to represent it as a structured, unitary organization, as a subject and, if possible, to turn it into one. "I was speaking with a leader of the Movement; first of all, he rejects the term 'leader': they have no leaders. [...] The Movement, he says, is an elusive mobility, a ferment of tendencies, of groups and sub-groups, an assemblage of autonomous molecules. [...] To me, there is indeed a ruling group to the Movement; it is an 'internal' group, insubstantial in appearance but in reality perfectly structured. Rome, Bologna, Turin, Naples: there is indeed a concerted strategy. The ruling group remains invisible and public opinion, however well informed, is in no position to judge." ("The Autonomists' Paleo-Revolution," *Corriere della Sera*, May 21, 1977). No one will be surprised to learn that Empire recently tried the same thing to counter the return of the anti-capitalist offensive, this time targeting the mysterious "Black Blocs." Although the Black Bloc has never been anything but a protest *technique* invented by German Autonomists in the 1980s, then improved on by American anarchists in the early 1990s—a *technique*, that is, something reappropriable, infectious—Empire has for some time spared no effort dressing it up as a subject in order to turn it into a closed, compact, foreign entity. "According to Genovese magistrates, Black Blocs make up 'an armed gang' whose horizontal, nonhierarchical structure is composed of independent groups with no single high command, and therefore able to save itself 'the burden of centralized control,' but so dynamic that it is capable of 'developing its own strategies' and making 'rapid, collective decisions on a large scale' while maintaining the autonomy of single movements. This is why it has achieved 'a political maturity that makes Black Blocs a real force'" ("Black Blocs Are an Armed Gang," *Corriere della Sera*, August 11, 2001). Desperately compensating for its inability to achieve any kind of ethical depth, Empire constructs for itself the fantasy of an enemy it is capable of destroying.

In attempting to counter subversion it is necessary to take account of three separate elements. The first two constitute the target proper, that is to say the Party or Front and its cells and committees on the one hand, and the armed groups who are supporting them and being supported by them on the other. They may be said to constitute the head and body of a fish. The third element is the population and this represents the water in which the fish swims. Fish vary from place to place in accordance with the sort of water in which they are designed to live, and the same can be said of subversive organizations. If a fish has got to be destroyed it can be attacked directly by rod or net, providing it is in the sort of position which gives these methods a chance of success. But if rod and net cannot succeed by themselves it may be necessary to do something to the water which will force the fish into a position where it can be caught. Conceivably it might be necessary to kill the fish by polluting the water, but this is unlikely to be a desirable course of action.

— Frank Kitson, *Low Intensity Operations: Subversion, Insurgency and Peacekeeping*, 1971[34]

Frattanto i pesci, / di quali discendiamo tutti, / assistettero curiosi / al dramma personale e collettivo / di questo mondo che a loro / indubbiamente doveva sembrare cattivo / e cominciarono a pensare, nel loro grande mare /

come è profondo il mare. / È chiaro che il pensiero fa
paura e dà fastidio / anche se chi pensa è muto come un
pesce / anzi è un pesce / e come pesce è difficile da bloccare
perché lo protegge il mare / come è profondo il mare [...]
— Lucio Dalla, *Come è profondo il mare*, 1977[35]

Empire's reconfiguration of hostilities has largely gone unnoticed. It has gone unnoticed because it first appeared outside metropolises, in former colonies. The prohibition on war—a simple declaration with the League of Nations that became actual with the invention of nuclear weapons—produced a decisive transformation of war, a transformation that Schmitt attempted to account for with his concept of "global civil war." Since all war between states has become criminal with respect to the world order, not only do we now see only limited conflicts, but the very nature of the enemy has changed: *the enemy has been domesticated.* The liberal state has folded into Empire to such an extent that even when the enemy is identified as a state, a "rogue state" in the cavalier terminology of imperial diplomats, the war waged against it now takes the form of a simple police operation, a matter of in-house management, a law and order initiative.

Imperial war has neither a beginning nor an end, it is a permanent process of pacification. The essential aspects of its methods and principles have been known for fifty years. They were developed in the wars of decolonization during which the oppressive state apparatus underwent a decisive change. From then on the enemy was no longer an isolable entity, a foreign nation, or a determined class; it was somewhere lying in ambush within the population, with no visible attributes. If need be, it was the population *itself*, the population as insurgent force. The configuration of hostilities specific to the Imaginary Party thus immediately revealed itself in the guise of guerilla warfare, of partisan war. Consequently, not only has the army become the police, but the enemy has become a "terrorist"—the resistance to the German occupation was a "terrorist" activity; the Algerian insurgents opposing the French occupation, "terrorists"; the anti-imperial militants of the 1970s, "terrorists"; and, today, those all-too-determined elements of the anti-globalization movement, "terrorists." Trinquier, one of the chief architects as well as a theoretician of the Battle of Algiers: "The job of pacification devolving on the military would create problems that it was not accustomed to have to solve. Exercising police powers in a large city was not something it knew well how to do. The Algerian rebels used a new weapon for the first time: *urban terrorism*. [...] It offers an incomparable advantage, but it has one serious drawback: the population that harbors the terrorist knows him. At any time, given the opportunity, it might denounce him to the authorities. Strict control of the population can rob him of this vital source of support" (*Le Temps perdu*).[36] Historical conflict hasn't followed the principles of classical warfare for over a half-century; for more than a half-century now there have been only *extraordinary wars*.

It is these extraordinary wars, these irregular forms of war without principles, that have gradually dissolved the liberal state into the Imaginary Party. All the counterinsurgency doctrines—those of Trinquier, Kitson, Beauffre, Colonel Château-Jobert—are categorical on this point: the only way to fight guerilla warfare, to fight the Imaginary Party, is to employ its techniques. "One must operate like a partisan wherever there are partisans." Again, Trinquier: "But he must be made to realize that, when he [the insurgent] is captured, he cannot be treated as an ordinary criminal, nor as a prisoner taken on the battlefield. [...] No lawyer is present for such an interrogation. If he gives the information requested, the examination is quickly terminated; if not, specialists must force his secret from him. Then, as a soldier, he must face the suffering, and perhaps the death, he has heretofore managed to avoid. The terrorist must accept this as a condition inherent in his trade and in his methods of warfare that, with full knowledge, his superiors and he himself have chosen" (*Modern Warfare*).[37] The continuous surveillance of the population, the labeling of at-risk dividuals, legalized torture, psychological warfare, police control of Publicity, the social manipulation of affects, the infiltration and exfiltration of "extremist groups," the state-run massacre, like so many other aspects of the massive deployment of imperial apparatuses, respond to the necessities of uninterrupted war, most often carried out without a fuss. For as Westmoreland said: "A military operation is only one of a variety of ways to fight the communist insurgency" ("Counterinsurgency," *Tricontinental*, 1969).

In the end, only partisans of urban guerilla warfare have understood what the wars of decolonization were all about. Modeling themselves on the Uruguayan Tupamaros, they alone grasped the *contemporary* stakes in the conflicts of "national liberation." They alone, and the imperial forces. The chairman of a seminar on "The Role of the Armed Forces in Peace-Keeping in the 1970s," held by the Royal United Services Institute for Defence Studies in London in April 1973, declared, "if we lose in Belfast we may have to fight in Brixton or Birmingham. Just as in Spain in the thirties was a rehearsal for a wider European conflict, so perhaps what is happening in Northern Ireland is a rehearsal of urban guerilla war more widely in Europe and particularly in Great Britain."[38] All the current pacification campaigns, all the activities of "international peacekeeping forces" currently deployed on the outskirts of Europe and throughout the world, obviously foreshadow other "pacification campaigns," this time on European territory. Only those who fail to understand that their role is to *train people struggling against us* seek in some mysterious worldwide conspiracy the reason for these operations. No personal trajectory better sums up the expansion of external pacification to domestic pacification than that of the British officer Frank Kitson, the man who established the strategic doctrine thanks to which the British state defeated the Irish insurgency and NATO the Italian revolutionaries. Thus Kitson, before confiding his doctrine in *Low Intensity Operations: Subversion, Insurgency and Peacekeeping*, took part in the decolonization wars in Kenya against the Mau-Mau, in Malaysia against the communists, in Cyprus against Grivas, and, finally, in Northern Ireland. From his doctrine we will focus on only a bit of first-hand information concerning imperial rationality. We will condense them to three postulates. The first is that there is absolute continuity between the pettiest crimes and insurgency proper. For Empire, war is a continuum— *warfare as a whole*, says Kitson; it is necessary to respond from the very first "incivility" to whatever threatens the social order and in so doing to ensure the "integration of military, police, and civil activities at every level." Civilian-military integration is the second imperial postulate. Because during the time of nuclear pacification wars between states became increasingly rare and because the essential job of the army was no longer external but domestic warfare, counterinsurgency, it was advisable to accustom the population to a permanent military presence in public spaces. An imaginary terrorist threat—Irish or Muslim—would justify regular patrols of armed men in train stations, airports, subways, etc. In general, one would look to multiply the points of indistinction between civilians and the military. The computerization of the social sphere, that is, the fact that every movement tends to produce information, is at the heart of this integration. The proliferation of diffuse surveillance apparatuses, of tracing and recording, serves to generate an abundance of low-grade intelligence on which the police can then base its activities. The third principle of imperial action following this preparatory insurrectionary phase—which is the normal political situation—involves "peace movements." As soon as violent opposition to the existing order arises, peace movements among the population must be accommodated if not created out of whole cloth. Peace movements serve to isolate the rebels while they are infiltrated in order to make them commit acts that discredit them. Kitson explains the strategy, employing the poetic formula, "drowning the baby in its own milk." In any event, it is never a bad idea to brandish an imaginary terrorist threat in order to "make the living conditions of the population sufficiently uncomfortable that they create a stimulus to return to normal life." If Trinquier had the honor of advising American counterinsurgency bigshots, the man who in 1957 had already established a vast system of neighborhood policing, of controlling the Algiers population, a system given the modernist name "Urban Security Apparatus," Kitson for his part saw his work reach the highest circles of NATO. He himself quickly joined the Atlanticist organization. Hadn't that always been his calling? He who hoped that his book would "draw attention to the steps which should be taken now to make the army ready to deal with subversion, insurrection, and peace-keeping operations during the second half of the 1970s," which he concluded by emphasizing the same point: "Meanwhile it is permissible to hope that the contents of this book will in some way help the army to prepare itself for any storms which may lie ahead in the second half of the 1970s."[39]

Under Empire, the very persistence of the formal trappings of the state is part of the strategic maneuvering that renders it obsolete. Insofar as Empire is unable to recognize an enemy, an alterity, an ethical difference, it cannot recognize the war conditions it has created. There will therefore be no state of exception as such but a permanent, indefinitely extended state of emergency. The legal system will not be officially suspended in order to wage war against the domestic enemy, against the insurgents, or whatever else; to the current system will simply be added a collection of *ad hoc* laws designed to fight the unmentionable enemy. "Common law will thus transform into a proliferative and supererogatory development of special rules: the rule will consequently become a series of exceptions" (Luca Bresci, Oreste Scalzone, *Italia: la excepción es la regla* [*The Exception Is the Rule*]).[40] The sovereignty of the police, which have again become a war machine, will no longer suffer opposition. THEY will recognize the police's right to shoot on sight, reestablishing in practice the death penalty which, according to the law, no longer exists. THEY will extend the maximum time spent in police custody such that the charges will henceforth amount to the sentence. In certain cases, the "fight against terrorism" will justify imprisonment without trial as well as warrantless searches. In general, THEY will no longer judge facts, but persons, subjective conformity, one's aptitude for repentance; to that end, sufficiently vague qualifiers like "moral complicity," "illegal membership in a criminal organization," or "inciting civil war" will be created. And when that is no longer enough, THEY will judge by theorem. To demonstrate clearly the difference between accused citizens and "terrorists," THEY will invoke laws dealing with reformed criminals in order to allow the accused to dissociate himself from himself, that is, to become vile. Significantly reduced sentences will then be granted; in the contrary case, *Berufsverbote* will prevail, outlawing the exercise of certain sensitive professions that require protection from subversive contamination. And yet, such a set of laws, like the Reale law in Italy or the German emergency acts, only *respond* to an already declared insurrectional situation. A lot more heinous are the laws intended to arm the *preventative* fight against the war machines of the Imaginary Party. Unanimously ratified "anti-sect laws" will supplement "anti-terrorism," as happened recently in France, in Spain, and in Belgium; laws that prosecute—without concealing the intention to criminalize—every autonomous assembly of the false national community of citizens. Unfortunately, it may become increasingly difficult to avoid local excesses of zeal like the "anti-extremism laws" passed in Belgium in November 1998, which penalize "all racist, xenophobic, anarchist, nationalist, authoritarian, or totalitarian conceptions or aims, whether political, ideological, religious, or philosophical in nature, contrary [...] to the functioning of democratic institutions."

In spite of all that, it would be wrong to believe that the state will survive. In the global civil war, its supposed ethical neutrality no longer fools anyone. The tribunal-form itself, whether civil court[41] or the International Criminal Tribunal, is perceived as an explicit mode of warfare. It is the idea of the state as a mediation between parties that is falling by the wayside. The historical compromise—experimented with in Italy from the early 1970s but now a reality in all biopolitical democracies following the disappearance of all effective opposition on the classical political stage—has finished off the very principle of the state.

In this way, the Italian state failed to survive the 1970s, to survive diffuse guerilla warfare, or rather it didn't survive *as a state*, only as a party, *as a party* of citizens, that is, as a party of *passivity and police*. And this is the party that the passionate economic turnaround of the 1980s blessed with an ephemeral victory. But the total shipwreck of the state only really came when one man took power, took over the theatre of classical politics, a man whose entire program was specifically designed to jettison classical politics and put pure entrepreneurial management in its place. At that point the state openly took on the role of a party. With Berlusconi, it isn't a single individual who has taken power but a form-of-life: that of a narrow-minded, self-seeking, philofascist petty-entrepreneur from the North of Italy. Power is once again ethically-based—based on business as the only form of socialization after the family—and he who embodies it *represents* no one and certainly not a majority, but *is* a perfectly discernable form-of-life with which only a small fraction of the population can identify. Just as everyone recognizes in Berlusconi the clone of the neighborhood asshole, the perfect copy of the worst local parvenu, everyone knows that he was a member of the P2 Lodge that turned the Italian state into its own personal instrument. *This is how, bit by bit, the state sinks into the Imaginary Party.*

The repressive societies now being established have two new characteristics: repression is softer, more diffuse, more generalized, but at the same time much more violent. For all who can submit, adapt, and be channeled in, there will be a lessening of political intervention. There will be more and more psychologists, even psychoanalysts, in the police department; there will be more community therapy available; the problems of the individual and of the couple will be talked about everywhere; repression will be more psychologically comprehensive. The work of prostitutes will have to be recognized, there will be a drug advisor on the radio—in short, there will be a general climate of understanding acceptance. But if there are categories and individuals who escape this inclusion, if people attempt to question the general system of confinement, then they will be exterminated like the Black Panthers in the U.S., or their personalities exterminated as it happened with the Red Army Faction in Germany.
— Félix Guattari, *"Why Italy?"* [42]

You have divided all the people of the Empire—when I say that, I mean the whole world—in two classes: the more cultured, better born, and more influential everywhere you have declared Roman citizens and even of the same stock; the rest vassals and subjects.
— Aelius Aristides, *To Rome* [43]

If there is a heuristic virtue to Italy in terms of politics, it is that in general historical incandescence has the virtue of increasing the strategic legibility of an age. Still today, the lines of forces, the parties present, the tactical stakes, and the general configuration of hostilities are more difficult to discern in France than in Italy; and with good reason: the counterrevolution that was forcibly imposed in Italy twenty years ago has barely established itself in France. The counterinsurgency process has taken its time here, and has been given the luxury of concealing its real nature. Having made itself indiscernible, it has also made fewer enemies than elsewhere, or more thoroughly duped allies.

The most troubling thing about the last twenty years is without a doubt that Empire has managed to carve out from the debris of civilization a brand new humanity organically won over to its cause: *citizens*. Citizens are those who, at the very heart of the general conflagration of the social sphere, persist in *proclaiming* their abstract participation in a society that now only exists negatively, through the terror it exercises over everything that threatens to abandon it and, in so doing, *to survive it.* The accidents and the rationality that produce the citizen all point to the heart of the imperial enterprise: to attenuate forms-of-life, to neutralize bodies; and the citizen advances this enterprise by self-annulling the risk he represents to the imperial environment. This variable fraction of unconditional agents which empire deducts from each population forms the human reality of Spectacle and Biopower, the point of their absolute coincidence.

There is therefore a factory of the citizen, whose long-term implantation is Empire's major victory; not a social, or political, or economic but an *anthropological* victory. Certainly, no effort was spared in order to bring it off. It began with the offensive restructuring of capitalist modes of production in reaction, starting in the early 1970s, to the resurgence of worker conflict in factories and to the remarkable disinterest in work then manifesting itself among the younger generations following '68. Toyotism, automation, job enrichment, increased flexibility and personalization of work, delocalization, decentralization, outsourcing, just-in-time methods, project-specific management, the closure of large manufacturing plants, flextime, the liquidation of heavy industrial systems, worker consolidation— these are but aspects of the reforms of the modes of production whose main purpose was to restore capitalist power over production. The restructuring was everywhere initiated by advanced columns of employers, theorized by enlightened union bosses, and put in place with the approval of the principal union organizations. As Lama explained in *La*

Repubblica in 1976: "the left must, with purpose and a clean conscience, help to reestablish today's much diminished profit margins, even if it means proposing measures that prove costly to the workers." And Berlinguer would declare at the same time that "productivity is not the weapon of the employer," but "a weapon of the workers' movement for advancing a politics of transformation." The *effect* of restructuring was only superficially the objective: "to part simultaneously with oppositional workers and abusive petty tyrants" (Boltanski, *The New Spirit of Capitalism*).[44] The objective was rather to purge the productive center of a society in which production was becoming militarized, to purge it of all the "deviants," of all the at-risk dividuals, of all the agents of the Imaginary Party. It was, furthermore, through the same methods that standardization operated inside and outside the factory: by portraying targets as "terrorists." There was no other reason for the firing of the "Fiat 61" in 1979, which foreshadowed the imminent defeat of workers' struggles in Italy. It goes without saying that such actions would have been impossible had worker leadership not actively participated in them, the latter being no less interested than management in eradicating chronic insubordination, unruliness, worker autonomy, "all this constant sabotage, absenteeism, this ungovernable, deviant, criminal activity" which the new generation of workers had imported to the factory. Certainly no one was in a better position than the left to mould citizens; it alone could criticize this or that person for deserting "at a time when we are all called on to show our civic courage, each of us in our own job"—thundered Amendola in 1977, lecturing Sciascia and Montale.

For more than twenty years, there has therefore been an entire calibration of subjectivities, an entire mobilization of employee "vigilance," a call for self-control from all sides, for subjective investment in the production process, for the kind of creativity that allows Empire to isolate the new *hard core* of its society: citizens. But this result couldn't have been achieved had the offensive over work not been simultaneously supported by a second, more general, more *moral* offensive. Its pretext was "the crisis." The crisis not only consisted in making commodities artificially scarce in order to renew their desirability, their abundance having produced, in '68, all too obvious disgust. Above all, the crisis renewed Blooms' identification with the threatened social whole, whose fate depended on the goodwill of everyone. That is precisely what is at work in the "politics of sacrifice," in the call to "tighten our belts," and more generally, currently, to behave "in a responsible way" in everything we do. But responsible for what, really? for our shitty society? for the contradictions that undermine *your* mode of production? for the cracks in *your* totality? Tell me! Besides, this is how one is sure to recognize the citizen: by his individual introjection of these contradictions, of the aporias of the capitalist whole. Rather than fight against the social relations ravaging the most basic conditions of existence, the citizen sorts out his garbage and fills his car with alternative fuel. Rather than contributing to the construction of *another* reality, on Fridays after work he goes to serve meals to the homeless in a center run by slimy religious conservatives. And that is what he is going to talk about at dinner the next day.

The most simple-minded voluntarism and the most gnawing guilty conscience: these are the citizen's defining characteristics.

Rarely has an intellectual endeavor been more unwelcome, more vulgar, and more pointless than the one undertaken by the aspiring managers of socialized Capital in their first bullshit-inaugurating issue of the rag *Multitudes*. Of course, I wouldn't even mention a publication whose only reason for being is to serve as the theoretico-urbane showcase for the most disastrous of careerists, Yann Moulier-Boutang, were the rag's scope not to reach beyond the militant micocircles that stoop to reading *Multitudes*.

Always hanging on the latest shenanigans of their master, who in *Exile* sang the praises of the "inflationary biopolitical entrepreneur," the bureaucrats of Parisian Negrism attempted to introduce a positive distinction between Biopower and *biopolitics*. Identifying themselves with a nonexistent Foucauldian orthodoxy, they courageously rejected the category of Biopower—which was really too critical, too molar, too unifying. To this they opposed biopolitics as "that which envelops power and resistance as a new language which each day compels them to confront equality and difference, the two principles—political and biological—of our modernity."[45] Since, as it was, someone more intelligent, namely, Foucault, had already pronounced the truism that "there is power only between free subjects," these gentlemen considered the notion of Biopower all too extreme. How could a productive power, whose purpose is to maximize life, be all bad? And furthermore, how democratic is it to speak of Biopower—or even of Spectacle? And wouldn't doing so be a first step towards a kind of secession? "Biopolitics," Lazzarato in his pink tutu prefers to think, "is therefore the strategic coordination of these power relations such that the living produce greater force." And leave it to the imbecile to conclude with an exhilarating program announcing a "return of biopower to biopolitics, of 'the art of governing' to the production and government of new forms of life."[46]

Of course, no one could say that Negrists have ever been burdened by philological concerns. It is always a bit frustrating to have to remind them that the project of a guaranteed salary was, well before they struck on the idea, proposed by the para-Nazi intellectual movement led by Georges Duboin, a movement that during the Occupation inspired the "scientific" work of the group "Collaboration." Similarly, it is with great modesty that we remind these morons of the origin of the concept of biopolitics. Its first occurrence in French dates to 1960. *La Biopolitique* was the title of a short pamphlet by the peace-drunk Genevese doctor A. Starobinski. "Biopolitics acknowledges the existence of the purely organic forces that govern human societies and civilizations. These are indiscriminate forces that drive the human masses against each other and provoke the bloody conflicts between nations and civilizations which lead to their destruction and extinction. But biopolitics also acknowledges the existence of constructive and conscious forces in the life of societies and civilizations which protect them and open new and optimistic perspectives to humanity. The indiscriminate forces—Caesarism, brute force, the will to power, the destruction of the weakest by force or trickery, through pillage or plunder. [...] While accepting the reality of these facts in the history of civilizations, we will go further still and maintain that the reality of truth, justice, the love of the Divine and of one's neighbor, mutual aid, and human brotherhood exists. All those who share the ideal of brotherhood, all those who preserve in their heart the ideal of Goodness and justice work to protect the superior values of civilization. We must recognize that everything we have, that everything we are—our security, our education, our very possibility of existing—we owe to civilization. This is why our basic duty is to do everything we can to protect and save it. To that end, each of us must let go of our personal preoccupations, dedicate ourselves to activities that improve society, develop our spiritual and religious values, and actively participate in cultural life. I do not believe that this is difficult, though goodwill is especially called for. For each one of us, the thoughts and action of each one of us, has a role to play in universal harmony. Every optimistic vision of the future is therefore both a duty and a necessity. We mustn't fear war and the disasters which result, for we are already there, we are already in a state of war." The attentive reader will have noticed that we have stopped ourselves from quoting the passages from the pamphlet that advocate "eliminating from within [our society] everything that might hasten its decline," and the conclusion that "at the current stage of civilization, humanity must be united."[47]

But the good Genevese doctor is but a sweet dreamer compared to those who would usher biopolitics into the French intellectual universe for good: the founders of the *Cahiers de la politique*, whose first issue was published in 1968. Its director, its kingpin, was none other than André Birre, the grim functionary who went from the League of Human Rights and a great project for social revolution in the 1930s to Collaboration. The *Cahiers de la biopolitique*, the mouthpiece of the Organisation du Service de la Vie, also wanted to save civilization. "When the founding members of the 'Organisation du Service de la Vie' conferred in 1965, after twenty years of unflagging work to define their position regarding the current situation, their conclusion was that if humanity wants to continue evolving and reach a higher plane, in accordance with the principles of Alexis Carrel and

Albert Einstein, it must purposefully restore its respect for the Laws of Life and cooperate with nature instead of seeking to dominate and exploit it as it does today. [...] This way of thinking, which will enable us to reestablish order in an organic way and allow techniques to reach their full potential and demonstrate their effectiveness, is *biopolitical*. Biopolitics can provide us the understanding we lack, for it is at once the science and the art of using human knowledge according to the givens of the laws of nature and ontology which govern our lives and our destiny." In the two issues of *Cahiers de la biopolitique*, one thus discovers logical digressions on the "reconstruction of the human being," the "signs of health and quality," the "normal, abnormal, and pathological," among considerations entitled, "when women govern the world economy," "when international organizations open the way to biopolitics," or better yet, "our motto and charter in honor of life and service." "Biopolitics," we learn, "has been defined as the science of the conduct of states and human communities in light of natural laws and environments and the ontological givens that govern life and determine men's actions."

It should now be easier to understand why the Negrists of *Vacàrme* not long ago called for a "minor biopolitics": because a major biopolitics, Nazism, wasn't, it seems, very satisfying. Thus the little Parisian Negrists' windy incoherence: if they were coherent, they may be surprised to find themselves suddenly the bearers of the imperial project itself, that of recreating an integrally engineered, finally pacified and fatally productive social fabric. But, luckily for us, these chatterers are clueless. All they are doing is reciting, to a techno beat, the old patristic doctrine of *oikonomia*, a doctrine which they know nothing about and have precisely no idea that the first millennium Church came up with it in order to found the limitless range of its temporal prerogatives. In patristic thought the notion of *oikonomia*—which can be translated in a hundred different ways: incarnation, plan, design, administration, providence, responsibility, office, compromise, dishonesty, or ruse—is what allows one to designate in a single concept: the relation of the divinity to the world, of the Eternal to historical development, of the Father to the Son, of the Church to its faithful, and of God to his icon. "The concept of economy is an organicist, functionalist one that simultaneously concerns the flesh of the body, the flesh of speech, and the flesh of the image. [...] The notion of a divine plan with the aim of administering and managing fallen creation, and thus of saving it, makes the economy interdependent with the whole of creation from the beginning of time. Because of this, the economy is as much Nature as Providence. The divine economy watches over the harmonious conservation of the world and the preservation of all its parts as it runs in a well-adjusted, purposive manner. The incarnational economy is nothing other than the spreading out of the Father's image in its historic manifestation. [...] The economic thought of the church thus constitutes at once an administrative and corrective way of thinking. It is administrative in that *oikonomia* is at one with the organization, management, and development of each ministry. But it is also necessary to add to its corrective function, because human initiatives that are not inspired by grace can only engender inequalities, injustices, or transgressions. The divine and ecclesiastical economy must therefore take charge of the wretched management of our history and regulate it in an enlightened and redemptive way" (Marie-José Mondzain, *Image, Icon, Economy*).[48] The doctrine of *oikonomia*, that of a final because original integration of all things—even suffering, even death, even sin—with divine incarnation is the declared program of the biopolitical project in so far as the latter is first of all a project for universal inclusion, for the total subsumption of all things in the boundless *oikonomia* of the perfectly immanent divine: Empire. In this way, when the magnum opus of Negrism, *Empire*, proudly identifies itself with an ontology of production, it is impossible to miss what our suit-clad theologian means: everything is *produced* in so far as it is the expression of an absent subject, of the absence of the subject, the Father, in virtue of which everything is—even exploitation, even counterrevolution, even state massacres. *Empire* logically closes with these lines: "Once again in postmodernity we find ourselves in [Saint] Francis's situation, posing against the misery of power the joy of being. This is a revolution that no power will control—because biopower and communism, cooperation and revolution remain together, in love, simplicity, and also innocence. This is the irrepressible lightness of and joy of being communist."[49]

"Biopolitics may very well lead to a revolt of the executives," bemoaned Georges Henein *in 1967*.[50]

Never has society *been as absorbed in the ceremonials of the "problem," and never has it been so democratically uniform in every sphere of socially-guaranteed survival. As differentiations between classes gradually fade, new generations "flower" on the same stalk of sadness and stupor, which is explained away in the widely publicized eucharist of the "problem." And while the most extreme leftism—in its most coherent form—calls for pay for everyone, capital caresses ever less modestly the dream of giving it what it wants: of purging itself of the pollution of production and allowing men the freedom to simply produce themselves as capital's empty forms, its containers, each one confronted with the same enigma: why am I here?*

— Giorgio Cesarano, *Manuale di sopravvivenza*
[Survival Manual] (1974)[51]

There is no need to refute Negrism. The facts do all the work. It is, however, important to frustrate the ways in which it will likely be used against us. The purpose of Negrism, in the last analysis, is to provide the party of the citizens with the most sophisticated ideology. When the confusion surrounding the obviously reactionary character of Bovism[52] and ATTAC finally lifts, Negrism will step forward as the last possible socialism, cybernetic socialism.

Of course, it is already amazing that a movement opposed to "neo-liberal globalization" in the name of a "duty to civilization"—which pities "young people" for being held in a "state of infra-citizenship" only finally to spew forth that /to answer the challenge of social disintegration and political desperation demands redoubling civic and activist efforts" /(*Tout sur ATTAC*)[53]—can still pass for representing any kind of opposition to the dominant order. And if it distinguishes itself at all, it does so only in the anachronism of its positions, the inanity of its analyses. Furthermore, the quasi-official convergence of the citizens' movement with lobbies advocating greater state control can only last so long. The massive participation of deputies, judges, functionaries, cops, elected officials, and so many "representatives of civil society," which gave ATTAC such resonance initially, has over time dispelled any illusions in its regard. Already the vacuity of its first slogans— "taking back our world's future together" or "doing politics differently"—has given way to less ambiguous formulas. "A new world order must be envisioned then built, one that embraces the difficult and necessary submission of all—individuals, corporations, and states—to the common interest of humanity" (Jean de Maillard, *Le marché fait sa loi: De l'usage du crime par la mondialisation*).[54]

No need for predictions here: the most ambitious in the so-called "anti-globalization movement" are already open Negrists. The three watchwords typical of political Negrism—for all its strength lies in its ability to provide informal neo-militants with issues on which to focus their demands—are the "citizen's dividend," the right to free movement ("Papers for everyone!"), and the right to creativity, especially if computer-assisted. In this sense, the Negrist perspective is in no way different from the imperial perspective but rather a mere instance of perfectionism within it. When Moulier-Boutang uses all the paper at his disposal to publish a political manifesto entitled "For a New New Deal,"[55] hoping to convert all the various Lefts of good faith to his project for society, he does nothing more than reiterate the truth about Negrism. Negrism indeed expresses an antagonism, but one *within the management class*, between its progressive and conservative parts. Hence its curious relationship to social warfare, to practical subversion, its systematic recourse to simply making demands. From the Negrist point of view, social warfare is but a *means* to pressure the opposing side of power. As such, it is unacceptable, even if it may be useful. Hence political Negrism's incestuous relationship with imperial pacification: it wants its reality but not its realism. It wants Biopolitics without police, communication without Spectacle, peace without having to wage war to get it.

Strictly speaking, Negrism does not coincide with imperial thought; it is simply the *idealist* face of imperial thought. Its purpose is to raise the smokescreen behind which everyday imperial life can safely proceed until, invariably, the facts contradict it. For this reason, it is again in its very realization that Negrism offers its best refutation. Like when an illegal immigrant gets a green card and then is satisfied with the most banal assimilation; like when the *Tute Bianche* got itself smacked in the face by an Italian police force with which they thought they had come to an understanding; like when Negri complains, at the end of a recent interview, that in the 1970s the Italian state was unable to distinguish among its enemies "those who could be rehabilitated from those who couldn't." Despite its conversion to Negrism, the citizens' movement is thus most certainly going to disappoint him. It is likely that a citizen's dividend will be established, and to a certain extent already is, in the form of welfare payments for political passivity and ethical conformity. Citizens, insofar as they are made to compensate more and more frequently for the failures of the welfare state, will be paid more and more overtly for their work in comanaging social pacification. A citizen's dividend will therefore be established as a form of coercion to maintain self-discipline, in the form of strange, extremely tight-knit, community policing. If necessary, THEY might even call it "existence wages," since it would in fact entail sponsoring those forms-of-life most compatible with Empire. As the Negrists predict, affects will be, indeed already are being "put to work": a growing proportion of surplus value is made from forms of work that require linguistic, relational, and physical skills that can only be acquired, not in the sphere of production, but in the sphere of reproduction; work time and life time are *effectively* becoming indistinguishable—but all that merely foreshadows the greater submission of human existence to the process of cybernetic valorization. The immaterial work that the Negrists present as a victory of the proletariat, a "victory over factory discipline," without question contributes to imperial aims, constituting the most underhanded of domesticating apparatuses, apparatuses for the immobilization of bodies. Proletarian self-valorization, theorized by Negri as the ultimate subversion, is also taking place but in the form of universal prostitution. Everyone sells himself as best he can, sells as many parts of his existence as he can, even resorts to violence and sabotage to do it, although self-valorization really only measures the self-estrangement that the value system has extorted from him, really only sanctions the massive victory of the system. In the end, the Negrist-citizen ideology will only serve to conceal in the Edenic attire of universal Participation the military requirement "to associate as many prominent members of the population, especially those who have been engaged in nonviolent action, with the government"

(Kitson),[56] the requirement to *make* them participate. That loathsome Gaullists of the Yolan Bresson[57]-type fight for more than twenty years for existence income, placing on it their hope for a "transformation of social life," should offer further proof of the true strategic function of political Negrism. A function that Trinquier, quoted by Kitson, wouldn't have denied: "The Sine Qua Non of victory in modern warfare is the unconditional support of the population."[58]

But the convergence of Negrism with the citizens' project for total control occurs elsewhere, not at the ideological but at the *existential* level. The Negrist, a citizen to this extent, lives in denial of obvious ethical facts by conjuring away civil war. But whereas the citizen works to contain every expression of forms-of-life, to conserve ordinary situations, to standardize his environment, the Negrist practices an extreme and extremely spirited ethical blindness. To him, everything is the same aside from the petty political calculations of which he occasionally avails himself. Those who speak of Negri's casuistry therefore miss the essential point. His is a veritable disability, a tremendous human deformity. Negri would like to be "radical" but he can't manage it. To what depth of the real, in fact, can a theoretician go who declares: "I consider Marxism a science whose employers and workers serve each other in equal measure, even if it is from different, opposite positions"? A professor of political philosophy who confides: "Personally, I hate intellectuals. I only feel comfortable with working-class people (especially if they are manual workers: in fact, I consider them among my dearest friends and teachers) and with businessmen (I also have some excellent friends among factory-owners and professionals)"? What is the sententious opinion worth of someone who fails to grasp the ethical difference between a worker and an owner, who regarding the businessmen of Le Sentier is capable of writing: "The new company manager is an organic deviant, a mutant, an impossible-to-eliminate anomaly. [...] The new union official, that is, the new type of company manager, doesn't worry about wages except in terms of social income"? Someone who confuses everything, declaring that "nothing reveals the enormous historical positivity of worker self-valorization better than sabotage," and recommends, for every revolutionary possibility, "accumulating a different capital"? Whatever his claims to playing the hidden strategist behind the "people of Seattle," someone who lacks the most elementary personal knowledge of himself and the world, the tiniest ethical sensitivity, can only produce disaster, reduce everything he touches to a state of undifferentiated flow, to shit. He will lose all the wars into which his desire to flee compels him, and in those wars he will lose those closest to him and, worse still, he will be incapable of recognizing his defeat. "All armed prophets have conquered, and unarmed ones fail. In the seventies, Negri might have understood this passage as a clarion call to frontal collisions with the state. Decades later, *Empire* offers by contrast an optimism of the will that can only be sustained by a millenarian erasure of the distinction between the armed and the unarmed, the powerful and the abjectly powerless" (Gopal Balakrishnan, "Virgilian Visions").[59]

*Starting in February something apparently inexplicable
had begun to shake the depths of Milan. A ferment, a kind
of awakening. The city seemed to be coming back to life.
But it was a strange life, an all too vigorous, too violent,
and above all too marginal one. A new city appeared to be
establishing itself in the metropolis. All over Milan, everywhere, it was the same story: bands of adolescents were
launching an attack on the city. First they occupied empty
houses, vacant shops, which they baptized "proletariat
youth circles." Then, from there, they spread out little by
little and "took over the neighborhood." It went from
theatrical performances to the little "pirate markets," not
to mention the "expropriations." At the height of the wave
there were up to thirty circles. Each had its headquarters,
of course, and many published small newspapers.*

*Milanese youth were passionate about politics and
the extreme-left groups, like the others, took advantage of
the renewed interest. More than politics, it was about culture, a way of life, a wide-ranging refusal of the status quo
and the search for another way of life. Milanese youth
nearly in their entirety were by then aware of everything
involving the student revolts. But unlike their elders they
loved Marx and rock and roll and considered themselves
freaks. [...] Fortified by their numbers and their despair,
the more-or-less politicized groups intended to live
according to their needs. The movie theaters being too*

expensive, certain Saturdays they used crowbars to impose a discount on tickets. They were out of money, so they launched a movement of tragically simple "expropriations," just short of looting. A dozen of them were enough to play the game, which involved entering a store en masse, helping oneself, and leaving without paying. The looters were called "the salami gang" because in the beginning they mainly raided delis. Very soon jean stores and record stores were also hit. By late 1976, expropriating had become a fad, and there were few high schoolers who hadn't tried it at least once. All classes were thrown together: the looters were as much the sons of factory workers as of the upper middle class and everyone united in a huge celebration that would soon turn to tragedy.
— Fabrizio "Collabo" Calvi, *Camarade,* P. 38 [60]

With the exception of a tiny minority of half-wits, no one believes in work anymore. No one believes in work anymore, but for this very reason faith in its *necessity* has become all the more insistent. And for those not put off by the total degradation of work into a pure means of domestication, this faith most often turns into fanaticism. It is true that one cannot be a professor, a social worker, a ticket agent, or security guard without certain subjective after effects. That THEY now call work what until recently was called leisure—"video game testers" are paid to play the whole day; "artists" to play the buffoon in public;

a growing number of incompetents whom THEY name psychoanalysts, fortune-tellers, "coaches," or simply psychologists get handsomely paid for listening to others whine—doesn't seem enough to corrode this unalloyed faith. It even seems that the more work loses its ethical substance, the more tyrannical the *idol* of work becomes. The less self-evident the value and necessity of work, the more its slaves feel the need to assert its eternal nature. Would there really be any reason to add that "the only real, true integration in the life of a man or a woman is that experienced through school, through the world of knowledge, and, at the end of a full and satisfying school career, through entering the workforce" (*Dealing with Uncivil Behavior in School*),[61] if the obvious reality weren't already breaking through? In any case, the Law gives up the game when it stops defining work in terms of an activity and starts defining it in terms of *availability*: by work THEY now only mean voluntary submission to the pure, exterior, "social" constraint of maintaining market domination.

Faced with these inescapable facts, even the Marxist economist loses himself in professorial paralogisms, concluding that capitalist reason is thoroughly unreasonable. This is because the logic of the present situation is no longer of an economic but of an ethico-political kind. *Work is the linchpin of the citizen factory*. As such, it is indeed necessary, as necessary as nuclear reactors, city planning, the police, or television. One *has to* work because one *has to* feel one's existence, at least in part, as foreign to oneself. And it is the same necessity that compels THEM to take "autonomy" to mean "making a living for oneself," that is, *selling oneself*, and in order to do so introjecting the requisite quantity of imperial norms. In reality, the sole rationality driving present-day production *is the production of producers*, the production of bodies that *cannot not work*. The growth of the cultural commodities industry, of the whole industry of the imagination, and soon that *of sensations* fulfills the same imperial function of neutralizing bodies, of depressing forms-of-life, of bloomification. Insofar as *entertainment* does nothing more than sustain self-estrangement, it represents a *moment* of social work. But the picture wouldn't be complete if we forgot to mention that work also has a more directly militaristic function, which is to subsidize a whole series of forms-of-life—managers, security guards, cops, professors, hipsters, Young-Girls,[62] etc.—all of which are, to say the least, anti-ecstatic if not anti-insurrectional.

Of the entire putrid legacy of the workers' movement nothing stinks as much as the culture, and now the cult, of work. It is this culture and this culture alone, with its intolerable ethical blindness and its professional self-hatred, that one hears groaning with each new layoff, with each new proof that *work is finished.* What one in fact ought to do is put together a brass band, which one could, for example, call the "Combo For the Death of Toil" (c.f.d.t.),[63] and whose purpose would be to turn up and play at each massive new layoff, marching to perfectly ruinous, dissonant, balkanized harmonies, and trumpeting the end of work and all the prodigious expanse of chaos opening up before us. Here as elsewhere, not to have come to terms with the workers' movement carries a heavy price, and the diversionary power that a gas factory like ATTAC represents in France has no other origin. Considering this, once one has grasped the central position of work in the manufacturing of the citizen, it isn't too surprising that the current heir to the workers' movement, the social movement, has suddenly metamorphosed into a *citizens' movement.*

We would be wrong to neglect the pure scandal, from the point of view of the worker's movement, created by practices through which the latter has obviously been surpassed by the Imaginary Party. First, because the privileged site of these practices is no longer the place of production but rather the entire territory; second, because they aren't the means to a further end—status, greater buying power, less work, or more freedom—but at once *sabotage and reappropriation.* Here again there is no historical context that offers us more insight into these practices, their nature, and their limits than the Italy of the '60s and '70s. The whole history of "creeping May" is in fact the history of the movement's being surpassed, the history of the extinction of "worker centrality." The incompatibility of the Imaginary Party with the workers' movement revealed itself for what it is: an *ethical* incompatibility. A blatant incompatibility, for example, in the *refusal to work* with which southern workers doggedly responded to factory discipline, thus shattering the Fordist compromise. It is to the credit of a group like Potere Operaio that it zealously brought the "war on work" into the factories. "The refusal to work and alienation from work are not occasional," observed the *Gruppo Gramnsci* in the early '70s, "but rooted in an objective class condition that the growth of capitalism ceaselessly reproduces and at ever higher levels: the new strength of the working class stems from its concentration and its homogeneity, stems from the fact that the capitalist relation extends beyond the traditional factory (and in particular to what is called the 'service sector'). In this way, it produces resistance, goals, and behaviors there as well, all tendentially based on the foreignness of capitalist work, and strips workers and employees of their residual professionalism, thus destroying their 'affection' for and any other kind of potential identification with the work that capital imposes on them." But it was only at the end of the cycle of worker struggles in 1973 that the Imaginary Party actually outstripped the movement. Indeed, at that point those who wanted to pursue the struggle had to recognize that worker centrality had ended and take the war out of the factory. For certain of them, like the BR, who stuck to the Leninist alternative between economic and political struggle, leaving the factory meant immediately launching oneself into the realm of politics, a frontal attack on state power. For others, in particular for the "autonomes," it meant the politicization of everything the workers' movement had forgotten: the sphere of reproduction. At the time, Lotta Continua came up with the slogan, "Take back the city!" Negri theorizes the "social worker"—a sufficiently elastic category to include feminists, the unemployed, the precarious, artists, the marginal, rebellious youth—and the "diffuse factory," a concept that justified leaving the factory because everything, in the last analysis, from the consumption of cultural commodities to domestic work, from then on contributed to the reproduction of capitalist society and, therefore, the factory was everywhere. In more or less short order, this change led to the break with socialism and with those who, like the BR and certain autonomous workers' groups, wanted to believe that "the working class in any case remains the central and governing nucleus of communist revolution" (BR—*Resolution of the Strategic Leadership*, April '75). The practices that brought about this ethical break immediately set at odds those who believed they belonged to the same revolutionary movement: autoreductions—in 1974, 200,000 Italian households refused to pay their electricity bills—proletarian expropriations, squats, pirate radio, armed protests, neighborhood struggles, diffuse guerilla warfare, countercultural celebrations, in short: Autonomia. In the midst of so many paradoxical declarations—it should still be recalled that Negri is the same schizophrenic who, at the end of twenty years of militancy focused on the "refusal to work," ended up concluding: "Therefore, when we spoke of the refusal to work, one should have understood a refusal to work in the factory"—even this dissociated personality, because of the radicalness of the period, happened to produce a few memorable lines like the following, taken from *Domination and Sabotage*: "The self-valorization-sabotage connection, like its opposite, prohibits us from ever having anything to do with 'socialism,' with its tradition, whether reformism or eurocommunism. It may even be the case that we are of a different race. We are no longer moved by anything belonging to the cardboard-cutout project of reformism, to its tradition, to its vile illusion. We are in a materiality that has its own laws, already discovered or still to be discovered through struggle—in any case, *different* laws. Marx's 'new mode of exposition' *has become the new mode of being of the class*. We are here, implacably, in the majority. We possess a method for destroying work. *We have sought a positive measure of non-work.* A positive measure of freedom from this shitty servitude which the bosses appreciate so much and which the official socialist movement has always imposed on us like a badge of honor. No, really, we can no longer say 'socialists,' we can no longer accept your ignominy."[64] What the Movement of '77 so violently came up against, a movement which was the scandalous, collective assumption of forms-of-life, was the workers' party, the party which *denigrates* every form-of-life. Thousands of prisoners allow us to gauge socialism's hostility toward the Imaginary Party.

The whole mistake of organized Autonomia, these "repulsive louses who aren't sure whether to scratch the back of the social-democrats or that of the Movement" (*La rivoluzione* 2, 1977), was to believe that the Imaginary Party could be *recognized*, that an institutional mediation would be possible. And this is the same mistake of their direct heirs, *Tute Bianche*, who in Genoa believed that it was enough to behave like cops, to denounce the "violent elements," for the police to leave them alone. On the contrary, we have to start from the simple fact that our struggle is *criminal from the outset* and behave accordingly. Only a power struggle guarantees us something and above all a certain impunity. The immediate affirmation of a need or desire—in so far as it implies a certain knowledge of oneself—ethically contravenes imperial pacification; and it no longer has the justification of militancy. Militancy and its critique are both in different ways compatible with Empire; one as a form of work, the other as a form of powerlessness. But the practice that moves beyond all this, in which a form-of-life imposes its way of saying "I," is bound to fail if its impact isn't worked out in advance. "Reestablishing the paranoid scene of politics, with its paraphernalia of aggressiveness, voluntarism, and repression, always runs the risk of stifling and repelling reality, that which exists, the revolt that emerges from the transformation of everyday life and from the break with mechanisms of constraint" (*La rivoluzione* 2).

It was Berlinguer, then head of the PCI, who shortly before the Bologna congress in September '77 uttered these historic words: "It is not some plague-victims (*untorelli*) who will destroy Bologna." He summarized Empire's opinion of us: we are *untorelli*, contagious agents, only good for extermination. And in this war of annihilation we should fear the worst from the left, because the left is the official trustee of the faith in work, of the particular fanaticism for negating all ethical difference in the name of an ethics of production. "We want a society of work and not a society of those aided by the state," Jospin, that lump of Calvinist-Trotskyite unhappiness, replied to the "Jobless Movement." The credo exemplifies the dismay of a being, the Worker, whose only sense of something beyond production lies in degradation, leisure, consumption, or self-destruction, a being that has so utterly lost contact with its own inclinations that it breaks down if not moved by some external necessity, by some *finality*. We should recall, for the occasion, that commercial activity, when it appeared as such in ancient societies, couldn't be named by itself since it was not only deprived of ethical substance but the very deprivation was raised to the level of an autonomous activity. It could therefore only be defined negatively, as a lack of *scholè* for the Greeks, *a-scholia*, and a lack of *otium* for the Latins, *neg-otium*. And it is still—with its celebrations, with its protests *fine a se stesso*, with its armed humor, its science of drugs, and its dissolving temporality—this old *art of nonwork* in the Movement of '77 that makes Empire tremble the most.

What else, in the end, makes up the plane of consistency on which our lines of flight emerge? Is there any other precondition to developing play among forms-of-life, any other precondition to communism?

"A critical metaphysics could emerge as a science of apparatuses..."

This text represents the founding act of S.A.C.S., the Society for the Advancement of Criminal Science. S.A.C.S. is a nonprofit organization whose mission is to anonymously collect, classify, and share all knowledge-powers that may be of use to anti-imperial war machines. (sasc@boum.org)

The first philosophies provide power with its formal structures. More specifically, "metaphysics" designates that apparatus wherein action requires a principle to which words, things, and deeds can be related. In the age of the Turning, when presence as ultimate identity becomes presence as irreducible difference, action appears without principle.

— Reiner Schürmann, *What is to be done with the end of metaphysics?*[1]

It may begin like this: there would be the sight, on a floor in one of these sinister glass hives of the service sector, this interminable scene, through panopticized space, of dozens of *settled* bodies, all in a row, arranged according to modular logic, dozens of apparently lifeless bodies, separated by thin glass walls, tapping away on their computers. Within the scene would in turn come the revelation of the brutally *political* character of this frantic immobilization of bodies. And the obvious paradox of bodies growing stiller the more their mental functions are activated, captivated, mobilized, the more their mental functions seethe, responding in real time to the fluctuations of the information flow streaming across the screen. Let us take this scene or rather *what we find there* and bring it with us as we stroll through an exhibition at the New York MOMA, where enthusiastic cyberneticists, newly converted to the alibi of art, have presented to the public all the apparatuses of neutralization, of normalization through work that they have in mind for the future. The exhibition would be entitled *Workspheres*: we would be shown how an iMac transforms work into leisure, work in itself having become as superfluous as it is intolerable; how a "user-friendly" environment disposes the average Bloom[2] to endure the very bleakest existence and thereby maximize his social productivity; or how every inkling of anxiety, in Bloom, will pass once THEY[3] have integrated all the parameters of his physiology, his habits, and his character into a personalized workspace. The cumulative effect of these "scenes" would give one the sense that THEY have finally succeeded in *producing* consciousness, in producing body as waste, as inert and cumbersome mass, the condition, but above all the *obstacle*, to *purely cerebral* development processes. The chair, the desk, the computer: an apparatus. A productive enframing. A methodical enterprise of attenuating all forms-of-life. Jünger indeed spoke of a "spiritualization of the earth" but in a sense that *was less than celebratory.*

One can imagine a different genesis. This time, in the beginning, there would be a certain irritation, the irritation associated with the widespread use of surveillance equipment in stores and in particular the spread of metal detectors. There would be the slight anxiety as you pass through them wondering if they will go off, if you will be extracted from the anonymous stream of consumers and labeled "the undesirable customer," "the thief." This time, then, it would begin with the irritation—perhaps even the resentment—of occasionally getting nabbed, and the clear intuition that these apparatuses have been *running* for some time. That the task of surveillance, for example, is more and more exclusively entrusted to an army of security guards, who are *all eyes* since they are themselves former thieves. Who are, in every one of their movements, *walking apparatuses*.

Let us now imagine a beginning—this time, completely unlikely—for the least credulous among us. The only possible starting point in this case would be the question of *determinity*, because there is, inexorably, determination; but also because this inexorability can *also* mean a formidable freedom of play with determinations, an inflationary subversion of cybernetic control.

> In the beginning, there would be nothing, finally. Nothing but the refusal to play innocently even one of the games THEY have devised to beguile us.

And who knows, the

FEROCIOUS

desire

to create

vertiginous

ones of our own.

1

What exactly is the *Theory of Bloom*? An attempt to *historicize* presence, to record, for starters, the current state of our being-in-the-world. Other similar attempts preceded the *Theory of Bloom*, the most remarkable of which, after Heidegger's *The Fundamental Concepts of Metaphysics*, was certainly De Martino's *The World of Magic*. Sixty years before the *Theory of Bloom*, the Italian anthropologist offered what remains to this day an unequaled contribution to the history of presence. But whereas philosophers and anthropologists take that as their *endpoint*—with an account of where we are at with the world, with an account of our abasement—we concede the point only because it is from there that we *begin*.

A man of his times, De Martino seems to believe in the whole modern fairytale of the classical subject, of the objective world, etc. He thus distinguishes between two ages of presence, one common to the primitive "world of magic" and one to "modern man." The whole misunderstanding in the West with regard to magic, and more generally to traditional societies, De Martino essentially says, arises from the fact that we attempt to apprehend them from the exterior, starting from the modern presupposition of established presence, of guaranteed being-in-the-world, founded on a clear-cut distinction between self and world. In the traditional, magic world the frontier that defines the modern subject as a solid, stable substratum, confident in his being-there and before whom opens out a world brimming with objectivity, is still problematic. The frontier still has to be won, to be fixed; for human presence is always under threat, is experienced as in constant danger. And this instability places it at the mercy of every intense perception, every situation saturated with affects, every inassimilable event. In extreme cases, known by various names in primitive civilizations, being-there is totally engulfed by the world, by an emotion, by a perception. It is what the Malay call *latah*, the Tungus *olon*, certain Melanesians *atai*, and to which is related, among the same Malay, *amok*. In such states, singular presence fades, becomes indistinct from phenomena, breaks down into a simple mechanical echo of the surrounding world. Thus a *latah*, a body affected with *latah*, will place his hand over a flame following the vaguest gesture that one makes to do so oneself; or, suddenly finding himself face to face with a tiger, he will start to imitate it furiously, possessed by this unexpected perception. Cases of collective *olon* have also been reported. During a Russian officer's training of a Cossack regiment, the men, instead of executing the colonel's orders, suddenly began to repeat them in unison; and the more the officer heaped insults on the men and the more irate he became at their refusing to obey, the more they returned his abuse and mimicked his anger. This is how De Martino, using his approximate categories, describes *latah*: "Presence tends to remain focused on a certain content, beyond which it cannot go; as a consequence, it disappears, withdraws as presence. The distinction between presence and the world that makes itself present collapses."[4]

For De Martino, then, there is an "existential drama," the "historical drama of the magic world," which is a drama of presence; and all magic beliefs, techniques, and institutions exist in order to respond to the situation—to save, protect, or restore threatened presence. The latter are therefore endowed with special efficiency, with objectivity inaccessible to the classical subject. One of the ways in which the Mota natives overcome the crisis of presence provoked by a strong emotional reaction is thus to link the victim of such a reaction with the thing that caused it or something that symbolizes the cause. During a ceremony this thing is declared *atai*. The Shaman establishes a common destiny between these two *bodies* which are from then on inextricably, ritually linked, to the point that *atai* quite simply means *soul* in the native language. "Presence that is in danger of losing control masters itself by attaching its own problematic unity to that of the object," De Martino concludes. The commonplace practice of inventing an *alter ego* object for oneself is what Westerners term "fetishism," thereby refusing to understand that through magic "primitive" man reconstructs, recaptures a presence for himself. As he reenacts the drama of his disintegrating presence, although this time accompanied, supported by the Shaman—in trance, for example—he stages the disintegration in such a way that he regains control of it. What modern man so bitterly resents in the "primitive," after all, is not so much his practice of magic as his audacity in appropriating for himself a right that is judged obscene: that of *evoking* the lability of presence and in so doing of making it *participable*. For the "primitives" have found the *means* to overcome the kind of dereliction whose more familiar images are the hipster stripped of his cell phone, the petty-bourgeois family deprived of TV, the driver whose car has been scratched, the executive without an office, the speechless intellectual, or the Young-Girl[5] without her purse.

But De Martino commits an egregious error, a substantive error, no doubt inherent to *every anthropology*. De Martino misjudges the scope of the concept of presence; he still conceives of it as *an attribute of the human subject*, which inevitably leads him to oppose presence and "the world that makes itself present." The difference between modern and primitive man does not lie, as De Martino has it, in the fact that the latter may be *lacking* vis-à-vis the former, primitive man having not yet acquired modern man's certainty. Quite the contrary, it lies in the fact that the "primitive" displays a greater openness, greater *attention* to the COMING INTO PRESENCE OF BEINGS and, consequently, a greater vulnerability to its fluctuations. Modern man, the classical subject, doesn't represent a leap beyond the primitive, he is simply a primitive who has been made indifferent to the event of beings, who no longer knows how to heed the coming into presence of things, who is *poor in world*. In fact, all of De Martino's work is filled with an unhappy love for the classical subject. Unhappy because De Martina, like Janet, has an all too intimate understanding of the magic world, an all too rare sensitivity to Bloom not to experience fully, secretly, its effects. The only thing is, for a man in Italy in the forties, certainly one was better-advised to stifle this sensitivity and to dedicate one's unbridled passion to the majestic and henceforth *perfectly kitsch* plasticity of the classical subject. De Martino was thus driven to the comical position of denouncing the methodological error of wanting to apprehend the magic world from the standpoint of an already certain presence, all the while maintaining that presence as the horizon of reference. As a last resort, he made his own the modern utopia of an objectivity purified of all subjectivity and of a subjectivity freed of all objectivity.

In reality, presence is hardly an attribute of the human subject; it is what *is given*. "The phenomenon to bear in mind is neither being alone nor its mode of being present, but the entry into presence—an always new entry—whatever the historical apparatus in which the given appears" (Reiner Schürmann, *From Principles to Anarchy*).[6] This describes the ontological ek-stasis of human being-there, its co-belonging *to each lived situation*. Presence in itself is INHUMAN, an inhumanity that triumphs in the crisis of presence, when being imposes itself with overwhelming urgency. The donation of presence can then no longer be received; every form-of-life, that is, every way to *receive* this donation, vanishes. What must be historicized is not, therefore, the progress of presence toward final stability, but the different ways in which presence is given, the different *economies of presence*. And if today, in the age of Bloom, there is in fact a generalized crisis of presence, this is simply due to the ubiquity of the economy in crisis: the WEST'S MODERN HEGEMONIC ECONOMY OF CONSTANT PRESENCE. An economy characterized by the denegation of the mere possibility of its crisis through the use of the classical subject—master and measure of all things—as a menace in order to keep things in line. Bloom historially marks the end of the socio-magic effectiveness of this kind of blackmail, of this fairytale. The horizon of human existence once again comprises the crisis of presence, although THEY don't respond to it in the same way as in the traditional world, although THEY don't recognize the crisis as such.

In the age of Bloom, the crisis of presence becomes chronic and objectified through an immense accumulation of *apparatuses*. Each apparatus functions as an ek-sistential prosthesis which THEY administer to Bloom so that he is able to live within the crisis of presence, albeit unwittingly, and to remain there day after day without succumbing: a cell phone, a sedative, a shrink, a lover, a movie—all make for decent crutches provided they can be changed up often enough. Taken singularly, the apparatuses are so many bulwarks erected against the event of things; taken together, they constitute the icy veil that THEY lay over the fact that each thing, in its coming into presence, carries with it a world. The purpose: to maintain at all cost and everywhere the dominant economy by managing authoritatively, omnipresently, the crisis of presence; to establish globally *a present* opposed to the free play of comings into presence. In a word: THE WORLD GROWS HARD.

Since Bloom first penetrated the heart of civilization, THEY have done everything THEY can to isolate him, to neutralize him. Most often and already very biopolitically, he has been treated as a disease—first called *psychasthenia* by Janet, then *schizophrenia*. Today THEY prefer to speak of *depression*. Terms change, of course, but the sleight of hand is always the same: reduce those extreme manifestations of Bloom to purely "subjective problems." By defining him as a disease, THEY individualize him, THEY localize him, THEY isolate him such that *he can no longer be assumed collectively*, commonly.

On closer inspection, biopolitics has never had any other aim but to thwart the formation of worlds, techniques, shared dramatizations, *magic* in which the crisis of presence might be overcome, appropriated, might become a center of energy, a war machine. The rupture in the transmission of experience, the rupture in historical tradition exists, is vehemently maintained, in order to ensure that Bloom is always left— entirely driven back onto "himself," onto his own solitary derision—to his unbearable mythical "freedom." *Biopolitics holds a monopoly over remedies to presence in crisis, which it is always ready to defend with the most extreme violence.*

A politics that challenges this monopoly takes as its starting point and center of energy the crisis of presence, Bloom. We call this politics *ecstatic.* Its aim is not to rescue abstractly—through successive re/presentations—human presence from dissolution, but instead to create participable magic, techniques for inhabiting not a territory but *a world.* And this creation, this play between different economies of presence, between different forms-of-life, entails the subversion and the *liquidation* of all apparatuses.

Those who, as a final reprieve from their passivity, insist on calling for a theory of the subject must understand that in the age of Bloom *a theory of the subject is now only possible as a theory of apparatuses.*

2

For a long time I believed that what distinguished theory from, say, literature, was its impatience to transmit content, its special capacity to *make* itself understood. And that effectively defines theory, theory as the unique form of writing *that is not a practice*. Thus it is that the infinite has its origin in theory, which can say everything without ever saying anything at all, in the end, of any consequence—to bodies, that is. One will see clearly enough that our texts are neither theory, nor its negation, but simply *something else*.

What is the perfect apparatus, the model-apparatus that would eliminate all misunderstandings with regard to the very notion of apparatus? The perfect apparatus, it seems to me, is AUTHORITY. In it *maximum circulation coincides with maximum control*. Nothing moves that isn't both incontestably "free" and strictly classified, identified, individuated in exhaustive files of digitized registrations. A network endowed with its own fueling stations, its own police, its autonomous, neutral, empty, and abstract spaces, the highway system perfectly represents the territory, as if laid out in bands over the land, a heterotopia, the cybernetic heterotopia. Everything has been carefully parameterized so that *nothing happens*, ever. The undifferentiated daily flow is punctuated only by the statistical, foreseen, and foreseeable series of *accidents*, about which THEY keep us all the better informed as we never see them with our own eyes—accidents which are not experienced as events, as *deaths*, but as a passing disruption whose every trace is erased within the hour. In any case, THEY die a lot less on state highways than on the interstates, as the DOT reminds us. And it is hardly as if the flattened animals, noticed only in the slight swerve they induce in passing cars, remind us what it means to *LIVE* WHERE OTHERS *PASS*. No atom of the molecularized flow, none of the impervious monads of the apparatus needs us to remind it that it should *get moving*. The highway[7] system was made—with its wide turns, its calculated, signalized uniformity—solely in order to merge all types of behavior into a single one: the non-surprise, sensible and smooth, consistently steered toward a destination, the whole traveled at an average and regular speed. Still, the slight sense of absence, spanning the distance from end to end, as if one could stay in an apparatus only if struck by the prospect of getting out, without ever having really been in it, been *there*. In the end, the pure space of the highway captures the abstraction of all *place* more than of all distance. Nowhere have THEY so perfectly substituted places with *names* through their nominalist *reduction*. Nowhere is separation so mobile, so convincing, and armed with a vocabulary, road signs, less apt to subversion. Thus the highway: the *concrete* utopia of cybernetic Empire. And to think that some have heard of the "information superhighway" without sensing the total police surveillance to come.

The metro, the *metropolitan* network, is another kind of mega-apparatus—in this case, underground. Given that the passion for policing has, since Vichy, never left the RATP,[8] no doubt a certain consciousness along the same lines has pervaded its every level, right down to its foundations. Thus a few years ago, in the corridors of the Parisian metro, we had the privilege of reading a long RATP statement adorned with a regal-looking lion. The title of the statement, written in huge bold type, read: "WHOEVER ORGANIZES THE WORKPLACE CONTROLS IT." Whoever deigned to stop for a second learned of the intransigence with which the local Authority was ready to defend its monopoly over management of the apparatus. Since then, it would seem that the *Weltgeist* has again made progress, this time among its followers in RATP public relations, because every PR campaign is now signed "RATP, *l'esprit libre*." "*L'esprit libre*"—the strange fate of a phrase that has run from Voltaire to ads for new banking services[9] by way of Nietzsche—*having* one's mind free from care [*l'esprit libre*] more than *being* a free thinker [*un esprit libre*]: that is what Bloom in his hunger for Bloomification demands. *To have one's mind free*, that is: the apparatus takes over for those who submit to it. There is real comfort in this—the power to forget, until further notice, that one is in the world.

In each apparatus, there is a hidden decision. The Good Cyberneticists from the CNRS[10] spin it this way: "The apparatus can be defined as the realization of an intention through the implementation of planned environments" (*Hermès*, no. 25).[11] *Flow* is necessary to the maintenance of the apparatus, because it conceals this decision. "Nothing is more fundamental to the survival of shopping than a steady stream of customers and products," observe, for their part, the assholes of the Harvard Project on the City.[12] But ensuring the durability and management of the molecuralized flow, linking together the different apparatuses, demands an equivalency principle, a *dynamic* principle distinct from the norm common to each apparatus. The equivalency principle is merchandise. Merchandise, that is, *money*, which individualizes, separates all the social atoms, and places them alone before their bank accounts like Christians before their God; money, which at the same time allows us to continually enter every apparatus and, with each entry, to record a *trace* of our position, our traffic. Merchandise, that is, *work*, which holds the largest number of bodies within a certain number of standardized apparatuses, forces them to pass through them and to *stay* there, each body, through its curriculum vitae, arranging for its own traceability. For isn't it the case that working no longer means *doing* something so much as *being* something, and first of all being *available*? Merchandise, that is, the *recognition* thanks to which everyone self-manages their submission to the policing of qualities and maintains with other bodies a prestidigitatory distance, sufficiently large to neutralize but not large enough to exclude them from social valorization. Thus guided by merchandise, the flow of Blooms quietly *necessitates* the apparatus that contains it. A whole fossilized world still survives within this architecture; it no longer needs to celebrate sovereign power *since it is itself, now, the sovereign power*: it need only configure space, while the crisis of presence does the rest.

Under Empire, the classical forms of capitalism survive, but as empty forms, as pure conduits serving to maintain apparatuses. Although their persistence shouldn't fool us: they are no longer self-contained, for they have become a function of something else. THE POLITICAL NOW DOMINATES THE ECONOMIC. What is ultimately at stake is no longer the extraction of surplus value, but *Control.* Now the level of surplus value extracted solely indicates the level of Control, which is the local condition of extraction. Capital is no longer but a *means* to generalized Control. And if commodity imperialism still exists, it is above all as an imperialism of apparatuses that it makes itself felt; an imperialism that responds to a single necessity: the TRANSITIVE NORMALIZATION OF EVERY SITUATION. This entails increasing circulation *between* apparatuses, for circulation provides the best vector for universal traceability and the *order of flows*. Here again our Good Cyberneticists show their flair for a phrase: "In general, the autonomous individual, understood as having his proper intentionality, stands as the central figure of the apparatus. [...] The individual is no longer positioned, the individual positions himself within the apparatus."[13]

There is nothing mysterious about why Blooms submit so overwhelmingly to apparatuses. Why, on certain days, at the supermarket, I don't steal anything; whether because I am feeling too weak or I am just lazy: not stealing provides a certain comfort. Not stealing means completely disappearing in the apparatus, means conforming to it in order to avoid the violence that underlies it: the violence between a body and the aggregate of employees, surveillance personnel, and, potentially, the police. Stealing compels me to a presence, to an attention, to expose my bodily surface to an extent that, on certain days, it is just too much for me. Stealing compels me to *think my situation*. And sometimes I don't have the strength. So I pay; I pay for sparing myself the very experience of the apparatus in all of its hostile reality. I pay with my *right to absence*.

3

What can be shown cannot be said.
— Wittgenstein[14]

Saying does not stand over against what is said.
— Heidegger[15]

There is a materialist approach to language based on the idea that what we perceive is inseparable from what we know about what we perceive. *Gestalt* has long shown how, when we look at a confusing image, the fact that someone tells us that it represents a man seated on a chair or a half-opened can of food is sufficient for us to see those things. A body's nervous reactions and, obviously, therefore, its metabolism are closely linked to the entirety of its representations, even if they aren't directly dependent on them. Such must be assumed in order to determine less the value than the *vital significance* of every metaphysics, its impact in terms of forms-of-life.

Given that, imagine a civilization whose grammar would hold at its center, particularly in the use of the most common verb in its vocabulary, a kind of vice, a defect, such that everything would be perceived from not only a distorted perspective but in most cases a *morbid* one. Imagine the effect on the common physiology of its users, the mental and relational pathologies, the vital impairment to which they would be prone. Such a civilization would surely be unbearable, producing only disaster and desolation everywhere it spread. The civilization is Western civilization; the verb is quite simply the verb *to be*. The verb *to be* not in its auxiliary or existential uses— "such and such is"—which are relatively harmless, but in its attributive uses—"this rose *is* red"—and its use in identity statements—"the rose *is* a flower"— which make the most egregious falsifications possible. In the statement "this rose is red," for example, I don't attribute to the subject "rose" a predicate that inherently belongs to it, but instead a predicate of *my perception*: I am the one—who isn't color-blind, who is "normal"—who perceives this wavelength as "red." To say that "I perceive the rose as red" would already be specious. As for the statement, "the rose is a flower," it conveniently allows me to hide behind the classifying operation that *I* carry out. It would instead be better to say "I classify the rose as a flower"—which is the common wording in Slavic languages. It goes without saying, then, that the effects of the *is* of identity have an entirely different emotional impact when it allows one to say of a man with white skin, "he is white," of someone with money, "he is rich," or of a woman who enjoys a little freedom, "she is a slut." The point is not at all to condemn the supposed "violence" of such statements and thus to pave the way for a new language police, for a more expansive political correctness which would ensure that every sentence carries with it its own guarantee of scientificity. The point is rather to know what we are doing, what THEY are doing to *us* when we speak, and to know it *together*.

The logic underlying these uses of the verb *to be* has been termed *Aristotelian* by Korzybski; we call it, simply, "metaphysics," and in this we are not far from thinking, with Schürmann, that "metaphysical culture in its entirety reveals itself to be a universalization of the syntactic operation of predicative attribution." At work in metaphysics, and in particular in the social hegemony of the *is* of identity, is just as much the negation of becoming, of the *event* of things and beings—"I am tired? First of all, that doesn't mean much. For my tiredness is not mine; I am not the one who is tired. 'There is something tiring.' My tiredness is part of the world in the form of an objective consistency, of a limp thickness to things themselves, of the sun and the rising road, and the dust and the stones" (Deleuze, "Dires et profils," 1947).[16] Instead of the event ("there is something tiring"), the metaphysical grammar compels us to state a subject then to refer it to its predicate: "I am tired"—a covert position, the omission of being-in-situation, a position that effaces the form-of-life expressing itself behind its utterance, behind the autarkic pseudo-symmetry of the subject-predicate relation. Naturally, the justification of such an evasion opens *Phenomenology of Spirit*, the cornerstone of the West's repression of determinity and forms-of-life, the manual to all future absence. "To the question: 'What is Now?'" writes our Bloom-in-chief, "let us answer, e.g. 'Now is Night.' In order to test the truth of this sense-certainty a simple experiment will suffice. We write down this truth; a truth cannot lose anything by being written down, any more than it can lose anything through our preserving it. If *now, this noon*, we look again at the written truth we shall have to say that it has become stale."[17] The crude sleight-of-hand here consists in reducing, as if innocuously, the enunciation to the utterance, in postulating the equivalence of the utterance made by a body in situation, the utterance *as event*, and the objectified, written utterance, which persists *as a trace* regardless of the situation. In either case, here time, *presence* are written off. In his last work, whose title, *On Certainty*, sounds like a kind of response to the first chapter of *Phenomenology of Spirit*, Wittgenstein considers the question further. From §588: "But don't I use the words 'I know that...' to say that I am in a certain state, whereas the mere assertion 'that is a...' does not say this? And yet one often does reply to such an assertion by asking 'how do you know?'—'But surely, only because the fact that I assert this gives to understand that I think I know it.'—This point could be made in the following way: In a zoo there might be a notice 'this is a zebra'; but never 'I know that this is a zebra.' 'I know' has meaning only when it is uttered by a person."[18]

The power that has made itself the heir of Western metaphysics, Empire draws its entire strength as well as the enormity of its weakness from this same metaphysics. Through the plethora of control devices, of continuous-tracking equipment with which it has covered the globe, through its very excess, it betrays the excess of its blindness. The mobilization of all these "intellects" which it prides itself on counting among its ranks only confirms its stupidity. It is striking to see, year in, year out, how beings increasingly slip between their predicates, between the identities that THEY give them. As surely as ever, Bloom makes progress. Everything becomes indistinguishable. THEY find it increasingly difficult to make "an intellectual" of those who think, "a wage-earner" of those who work, "a murderer" of those who kill, "an activist" of those who engage in activism. Formalized language, the arithmetic of the norm, has no hold on substantial distinction. Bodies no longer allow themselves to be reduced to the qualities that THEY intended to assign to them. Bodies refuse to *incorporate* them. They silently slip away. Recognition, which first designates *a certain distance between bodies*, is overrun at every point. It can no longer account for what is really happening *between bodies*. Thus the need for apparatuses, more and more apparatuses: in order to stabilize the relationship between predicates and "subjects" that stubbornly elude them; to thwart the diffuse creation of complex, asymmetric, perverse relationships with those predicates; to produce information, to produce the real *as information*. Clearly, the deviations measured by the norm, those according to which THEY individualize-apportion bodies, are no longer enough to maintain order; in addition, terror must be made to reign, terror of straying *too far* from the norm. A completely new policing of qualities, an entirely ruinous network of microsurveillance, of microsurveillance of every instant and every space, have become necessary to ensure the artificial stability of an imploding world. Attaining universal self-control demands a completely new densification. Mass dissemination of always more integrated, always more insidious control apparatuses. "The Apparatus: Helping Identities in Crisis," write the fuckers at CNRS.[19] But regardless of what THEY do to ensure the dreary linearity of the subject-predicate relation in order to submit all being to its representation, despite their historial detachment, despite *Bloom*, it is no use. Apparatuses may very well fix, conserve outmoded economies of presence, make them last beyond their event, they cannot stop *the seat of phenomena*, which will, sooner or later, overwhelm them. For now, the fact that most often it isn't being [*étant*] that possesses the qualities we attach to it, but rather our perception, which always shows itself most clearly in our metaphysical poverty, the poverty *of our ability to perceive*, makes us experience everything as having no qualities, makes us *produce the world as devoid of qualities*. In this historial collapse, things themselves, free of all attachments, come more and more urgently into presence.

Indeed, it is as an *apparatus* that each detail of the world appears to us—a world which has become foreign, precisely, in each of its details.

4

Our reason is the difference of discourses,
our history the difference of times,
our selves the difference of masks.
— Michel Foucault, *Archeology of Knowledge*[20]

It is characteristic of an abruptly major thought to *know what it is doing*, to know *in which operations it is involved*. Not in view of reaching some final, cautious, and measured Reason, but rather in order to *intensify* the dramatic pleasure of the play of existence even in its very inevitabilities. This is obscene, of course. And I have to say that, wherever one goes, in whatever circle one runs, every thought *of the situation* is immediately understood and conjured away as a perversion. To forestall this unfortunate reaction, there is always, of course, at least one respectable way out, which is to pass the thought off as a *critique*. In France, by the way, this is something THEY are more than eager to do. By revealing my hostility to a thing whose functions and determinisms I have grasped, I protect the very thing I want to destroy *from myself, from my practice*. And that—this innocuousness—is exactly what THEY expect when they urge me to declare myself a critic.

The freedom of play that follows from the acquisition of knowledge-power terrifies everyone everywhere. Empire continuously exudes this terror—terror of crime—among bodies, thus ensuring its monopoly over knowledge-powers, that is, in the end, its monopoly over *all power*. Domination and Critique have always formed an apparatus covertly directed against a common *hostis*: the conspirator, who works *under cover*, who uses everything THEY give him and everything THEY attribute to him *as a mask*. The conspirator is everywhere hated, although THEY will never hate him as much as he *enjoys* playing his game. No doubt a certain amount of what one usually calls "perversion" accounts for the pleasure, since what he enjoys, among other things, is his opacity. But that isn't the reason THEY continue to push the conspirator to make himself a critic, to *subjectivate* himself as critic, nor the reason for the hate THEY so commonly express. The reason is quite simply the *danger* he represents. The danger, for Empire, is war machines: that one person, that people transform themselves into war machines, ORGANICALLY JOIN THEIR TASTE FOR LIFE AND THEIR TASTE FOR DESTRUCTION.

The moralizing at the heart of every critique should not, in its turn, be critiqued; we need only recognize how little penchant we have for what is in fact at work: a love exclusively of sad affects, impotence, contrition; a desire to *pay*, to atone, to be punished; a passion for accusations; a hatred of the world, of life; the herd instinct; the expectation of martyrdom. The whole business of "conscience" has never truly been understood. There is in fact a *necessity* to conscience that is in no way a necessity to "rise up," but a necessity to raise, to refine, to spur *our pleasure*, to intensify *our enjoyment*. A science of apparatuses, a critical metaphysics is thus truly necessary, but not in order to sketch out some kind of pretty certainty to hide behind, nor even to *add* to life the thought of such a certainty, as some have said. We need to think our life in order to *intensify* it dramatically. What do I care about a refusal if it isn't at the same time a meticulous understanding of destruction? What do I care about knowledge that doesn't increase my strength—which THEY hypocritically call "lucidity"?

As for apparatuses, the vulgar tendency—of a body *that knows nothing of joy*—would be to reduce the present revolutionary perspective to the prospect of their immediate destruction. Apparatuses would thus provide a kind of scapegoat about which everyone could once again thoroughly agree. And we would revive the oldest of modern fantasies, the romantic fantasy that closes *Steppenwolf*: that of a war of men against machines. Reduced to that, the revolutionary perspective would once again be but an icy abstraction.

However, the revolutionary process is either a process of a general increase in power or it is nothing at all. Its Hell is the experience and science of apparatuses, its purgatory the distribution of this science and the flight from apparatuses, its Paradise insurrection, the destruction of apparatuses. And it falls *to each of us* to play out this divine comedy, like an irrevocable experiment.

For the time being the petit-bourgeois terror of language still reigns everywhere. On the one hand, in the sphere of "the everyday," THEY tend to take things for words, that is, apparently, *for what they are*—"a cat is a cat," "a penny is a penny," "I am me"—on the other hand, as soon as the THEY is subverted and language unleashed as an agent of potential disorder within the clinical regularity of the already-known, THEY cast it out into the nebulous regions of "ideology," of "metaphysics," of "literature," or, more commonly, of "bullshit." And yet there have been and there will be insurrectional moments when, under the effect of a flagrant denial of the everyday, common sense overcomes terror. THEY then understand that what is real in words is not what the words refer to—a cat is not "a cat"; a penny is less than ever "a penny"; I am no longer "myself." *What is real in language are the operations it performs.* To describe a being [*étant*] as an *apparatus*, or as being produced by an apparatus, *denatures* the given world, serves to *distance* us from the familiar, or at least that is what it is meant to do. But you know all this already.

Keeping the given world at a distance has until now been the characteristic feature of critique. Only critique believed that, once at a distance, the die was cast. For at bottom it was less important for critique to keep the world away than to keep itself out of the world's reach—and in some nebulous region. Critique wanted THEM to know its hostility to the world, its inherent transcendence. It wanted THEM to believe, to assume it operates elsewhere, in some Grand Hotel Abyss[21] or in the Republic of Letters. What matters to us is exactly the opposite. We impose a distance between us and the world, which is not to say that we could ever be elsewhere, but in order to *be in the world differently*. The distance we introduce is the space of play our gestures require; gestures that are engagements and disengagements, love and extermination, sabotage, abandon. The thought of apparatuses, critical metaphysics, prolongs a long-paralyzed critical gesture, prolongs it and in so doing *nullifies* it. In particular, it nullifies what, for more than seventy years, has stood as the center of energy of whatever life has been left in Marxism—I mean the famous chapter in *Capital* on "The Fetishism of Commodities and the Secret Thereof." Nowhere is it more lamentably obvious that Marx failed to think beyond the Enlightenment, that his *Critique of Political Economy* was nothing *but a critique*, than in these few paragraphs.

Marx came across the notion of fetishism as early as 1842, in his reading of that Enlightenment classic *Du Culte des Dieux-Fétiches* [*On the Worship of Fetish-gods*] by Charles de Brosses. Starting with his famous article on "Thefts of Wood," Marx compared gold to a fetish, basing the comparison on an anecdote taken from de Brosses's book. De Brosses invented the concept of fetishism, expanding the illuminist interpretation of certain African religions to all civilizations. For him, fetishism is the form of worship specific to "primitives" in general. "So many like facts, or those of similar kind, establish with the utmost certainty that as the Religion of African Negroes and other Barbarians is today, such was that of ancient peoples in earlier times; and that through the centuries, as well as throughout the world, we find this direct cult consecrated to animal and plant objects rejected." What most shocks the man of the Enlightenment, and especially Kant, in fetishism, is the way an African perceives things, which Bosman reports in *A New and Accurate Description of the Coast of Guinea* (1705): "We make and break our Gods, and [...] are the inventors and the masters of that to which we sacrifice." Fetishes are those objects or those beings, those *things*, in any case, with which the "primitive" magically links himself in order to restore a presence that some strange, violent, or simply unexpected phenomenon has made uncertain. In fact, the thing may be anything at all that the Savage "deifies directly," as the disgusted *Aufklärer* puts it, seeing only things and not the magic operation that restores presence. And if he can't see the operation, this is because *for him no less than for the "primitive"—except for the witch, of course—faltering presence, the dissolution of the self are inadmissible.* The difference between the modern and the primitive hinges solely on the fact that the former denies destabilized presence, having established himself *in the existential denegation* of his own fragility, whereas the latter accepts it providing a remedy is found at all cost. Thus the *Aufklärer*'s polemical—anything but easy—relationship with the "magic world," whose very *possibility* scares him to death. Thus, too, the invention of "madness," for those who refuse to submit to such harsh discipline.

In this first chapter of *Capital*, Marx's position is no different from Charles de Brosses's: the gesture is typical of the *Aufklärer*, of the critic. "Commodities have a secret, and I will reveal it. As you will soon see, they won't have their secret for long!" Neither Marx nor Marxism has ever got past the metaphysics of subjectivity, which is why feminism, or cybernetics, has had so little trouble undermining both. Because Marx historicizes everything *except human presence*, because he studies all economies *except those of presence*, he conceives of exchange value the way Charles de Brosses, in the eighteenth century, conceived of fetish religions among "primitives." He refuses to understand *what is at stake* in fetishism. He fails to see the *apparatuses* through which THEY make the commodity exist as commodity, how, materially—by accumulating *stock* at the factory; by orchestrating individuating *best-sellers* in a bookstore, a shop window or advertisement; by ruining the mere possibility of immediate use as well as that of any connection with places—THEY produce objects *as objects*, commodities *as commodities*. He acts *as if* everything that falls under sensible experience counted for nothing in his famous "fetish character," as if the idea of phenomenality that makes commodities as such exist weren't itself *materially produced*. Marx sets his misunderstanding of the classical-subject-with-guaranteed-presence, viewing "commodities as material, that is, as use values," against the general, indeed mysterious, blindness of the exploited. Even if he realizes that the latter must be in one way or another immobilized, made spectators to the circulation of things, in order for relations among them to resemble relations among things, he doesn't see the *apparatus* character of the mode of capitalist production. He fails to see what is happening, in terms of being-in-the-world, between these "men" and these "things." The very man who wants so badly to explain the necessity of everything doesn't understand the necessity of this "mystical illusion," its mooring in the vacillation of presence, *and in the suppression of this vacillation.* He simply dismisses the fact by attributing it to obscurantism, to theological and religious backwardness, to "metaphysics." "The religious reflections of the real world can, in any case, vanish only when the practical relations of everyday life between man and man, and man and nature, generally present themselves to him in a transparent and rational form."[22] So here we are: at the heart of the Enlightenment catechism, with everything programmatic that that implies for the world *such that it has been constructed ever since.* Since one cannot mention one's own relation to presence, the singular modality of one's being-in-the-world, nor that in which one is invested *here and now,* one inevitably draws on the same used-up tricks as one's predecessors: entrusting to a teleology—as implacable as it is derelict—to execute the sentence that one is in fact in the process of pronouncing. The failure of Marxism, like its historical success, is absolutely tied to the *classical* fallback position that it justifies, because, in the end, it remains within the fold of the modern metaphysics of subjectivity. A single discussion with a Marxist is enough to understand the real reason for his faith: Marxism serves as an existential crutch for many people who are scared that their world may not in fact be so self-evident. In the name of materialism, Marxism lets us smuggle in, draped in the robes of the noblest dogmatism, the most *vulgar* of metaphysics. There is no doubt that without the practical, *vital* contribution of Blanquism, Marxism alone would have been incapable of the October "Revolution."

Thus the task, for a science of apparatuses, isn't to denounce the fact that apparatuses *possess us*, that there may be *something magic* in them. It goes without saying that even behind the wheel we rarely actually act like drivers—and we don't need anyone explaining to us how a television, a PlayStation, or a "built environment" conditions us. *Instead, a science of apparatuses, a critical metaphysics, recognizes the crisis of presence and is prepared to compete with capitalism on the playing field of magic.*

WE WANT NEITHER VULGAR MATERIALISM NOR AN "ENCHANTED MATERIALISM"; WHAT WE ARE DESCRIBING IS A *MATERIALISM OF ENCHANTMENT*.

5

A science of apparatuses can only be *local*. It can only consist in the regional, circumstantial, and circumstanced mapping of how one or several apparatuses work. Totalization cannot occur without its cartographers' knowing, for rather than in forced systematicity, its unity lies in the question that determines its progress—the question: "*How does it work?*"

The science of apparatuses competes directly with the imperial monopoly over knowledge-powers. This is why its dissemination and communication, the circulation of its discoveries are essentially *illegal*. In this it should first of all be distinguished from *bricolage*, since the bricoleur accumulates knowledge of apparatuses only in order to improve their design, to turn them into a niche, that is, he accumulates all the knowledge of apparatuses *that is not power*. From the consensus point of view, what we call a science of apparatuses or critical metaphysics is finally nothing other than the science of crime. And here, as elsewhere, no initiation exists that isn't immediately experimentation, practice. ONE IS NEVER INITIATED INTO AN APPARATUS, ONLY INTO HOW IT WORKS. The three stages of this particular science are, successively: crime, opacity, and insurrection. Crime is the period of—necessarily individual—study of how an apparatus works. Opacity is the condition in which knowledge-powers acquired through study are shared, communized, circulated. Under Empire, the zones of opacity in which this communication takes place must by definition be seized and defended. This second stage therefore requires greater coordination. All s.a.c.s. activity is devoted to this opaque phase. The third level is insurrection, the moment when knowledge-powers and cooperation among forms-of-life—with an aim to destroying-enjoying imperial apparatuses—can be carried out freely, in the open air. Given our project, the present text can only serve as the most modest of introductions, passing somewhere between silence and tautology.

One begins to sense the necessity of a science of apparatuses as people, human *bodies*, finally settle into an entirely manufactured world. Few among those who find something wrong with the exorbitant misery that THEY would like to impose have yet really understood what it means to live in an *entirely produced* world. To begin with, it means that even what at first glance has seemed to us "authentic" reveals itself on contact as produced, that is, as possessing its non-production as a useful modality of general production. In terms of both Biopower and Spectacle, Empire consummates—I remember this run-in with a Negrist from *Chimères*,[23] an old hag in a gothic outfit (which wasn't bad), who claimed, as an indisputable gain for feminism and her materialist radicalism, that she hadn't *raised* her two children, but had *produced* them... it consummates the metaphysical interpretation of being [*étant*] as either being *produced* or nothing at all, produced, that is, caused to be produced in such a way that its creation and its ostension would be one and the same thing. Being produced always means *at once* being created and being made visible. In Western metaphysics, entering into presence has never been anything but entering into visibility. It is therefore inevitable that Empire, dependent on productive hysteria, should also be dependent on transparential hysteria. The surest way to prevent the free coming into presence of things is to induce it constantly, tyrannically.

Our ally—in this world given over to the most ferocious enframing, abandoned to *apparatuses*, in this world centered on fanatically controlling the visible, which is meant to be control of Being—our ally is none other than Time. *Time* is on our side. The time of our experience; the time that drives and rends our intensities; the time that breaks, wrecks, spoils, destroys, deforms; the time that is an abandon and an abandonment, that is at the very heart of both; the time that condenses and thickens into clusters of *moments* when all unification is defied, ruined, cut short, scratched out on the surface *by bodies themselves*. WE HAVE THE TIME. And whenever we don't have it, we can still give ourselves the time. To give oneself time: that is the condition to every communizable study of apparatuses. To identify the patterns, links, dissonances; each apparatus possesses its own little music, which must be put slightly out of tune, incidentally distorted, pushed to decay, to destruction, to become unhinged. Those who *flow* into the apparatus don't notice the music, their steps stick too close to the rhythm to hear it distinctly. For the latter, another temporality is needed, a specific rhythmicity, so that, although we enter the apparatus, we remain attentive to the *prevailing norm*. That is what the thief, the criminal learns: to unsync internal and external tempos, to split, to layer one's conscience, being at once mobile and static, on the lookout and deceptively distracted. To accept the dissolution of presence in the name of a simultaneous, asynchronous multiplication of its modalities. To turn the imposed schizophrenia of self-control into an offensive conspiratorial instrument. TO BECOME A SORCERER. "[T]o prevent this disintegration, one must go deliberately to the limit of one's own presence through a clearly-defined practice; one must go to the very essence of the outer limits and master it; the 'spirits' must be identified and evoked and one must develop the power to call upon them at will and profit professionally from their activity. These are the steps taken by the sorcerer; he transforms being-in-the-world's critical moments into a courageous and dramatic decision, that of establishing himself in the world. If being-in-the-world is taken as a *given*, it runs the risk of being dissolved: it has not yet been given. The magician, through the establishment of his vocation and successful initiation, *undoes* this presumed given and *reforms* it through a second birth; he goes to the limits of his presence in order to reform himself into a new and clearly-defined entity. The techniques he uses to increase the instability of presence, the trance itself and other related states, are the expressions of this being-there that disintegrates so that it may be reformed, the being that goes to the very end of its confines in order to discover itself as a sustained and guaranteed presence. The mastery that the magician has acquired allows him to penetrate not only his own instability, but also that in other people. The magician knows how to *go beyond himself*, not in the ideal sense, but actually, in the existential sense. The man whose being-there is made a problem and who has the power to establish his own presence, is not just an ordinary presence, but a being-there that makes itself present to others, understands their existential drama and influences its course."[24] Such is the starting point of the communist program.

Crime, contrary to what the Law implies, is never an act, a deed, but a *condition of existence*, a modality of presence, common to all agents of the Imaginary Party. To convince oneself, one need only think of the experience of theft or fraud, the elementary, and among the most routine—NOWADAYS, EVERYONE STEALS—forms of crime. The experience of theft is phenomenologically *other than* the so-called motives said to "push" us to it, and which we ourselves invoke. Theft is only a transgression from the point of view of representation: *it is an operation carried out on presence*, a reappropriation, an *individual* recovery of presence, a recovery of oneself *as a body in space*. The *how* of "theft" has nothing to do with its apparent legal occurrence. The *how* is the *physical* awareness of space and environment, the physical awareness of the *apparatus*, to which theft drives me. It is the extreme attention of the body illicitly on the subway, alert to the slightest sign of ticket inspectors. It is the nearly scientific understanding of the conditions in which I operate required for preparing a crime of some scope. With crime, there is a whole incandescence to the body, a transformation of the body into an ultrasensitive impact surface: that is its genuine experience. When I steal, I split myself into an apparent, unsubstantial, evanescent, absolutely nondescript [*quelconque*] presence and a second, this time whole, intensive, and internal presence in which every detail of the apparatus that surrounds me comes to life—with its cameras, its security guards, the security guards' *gaze*, the sightlines, the other customers, the way the other customers *look*. Theft, crime, fraud are the conditions of solitary existence at war with Bloomification, with Bloomification *through apparatuses*. The insubordination specific to the isolated body, the resolution to leave—even alone, even in a precarious way, through willful engagement—a certain state of stupefaction, half-sleep, self-absence: that is the essence of "life" in apparatuses. Given this, given this *necessary* experience, the question is how to move from there to conspiracy, to an actual circulation of illegal knowledge, an actual circulation of criminal science. It is the move to collective action that s.a.c.s. is here to facilitate.

6

Power speaks of "measures" [*dispositifs*]: national security measures, welfare measures, education measures, surveillance measures, etc. This allows it to give its interventions an air of reassuring insecurity. Then, as time dissolves the novelty of its introduction, the apparatus [*dispositif*] becomes part of "the order of things," and one only notices the insecurity of those drowned within it. The sellouts writing for the revue *Hermès*, particularly issue 25, didn't have to be asked to begin the work of legitimating this at once discreet and massive domination, which is capable of containing as well as distributing the general implosion of the social. "The social," they write, "seeks new regulatory methods to confront these difficulties. The apparatus [*dispositif*] is one attempt to do this. It helps to adapt to the fluctuation while at the same time delimiting it. [...] It is the product of a new way of articulating the individual and the collective, ensuring that a minimum of solidarity is maintained within a context of generalized fragmentation."[25]

Confronted with an apparatus, a turnstile in the Parisian metro, for example, the wrong question is: "why is it there?" and the wrong answer, in this particular case: "to prevent illicit behavior." The correct, materialist question, the *critical-metaphysical* question is rather: "what exactly does the apparatus do, what *operation* does it perform?" The response would then be: "The apparatus singles out, removes illicit bodies from the indistinct mass of 'users' by forcing them to move in an easily identifiable way (jumping over the turnstile or slipping in behind a 'legal user'). The apparatus in this way *gives life* to the predicate 'fare evader,' that is, it gives existence to a body defined *as a fare evader*." The essential thing here is the *as*, or more exactly the way in which the apparatus *naturalizes*, conjures away the *as*. For the apparatus has a way of making itself scarce, of *vanishing* behind the flow of bodies passing through it; its permanence depends on the continuous renewal of bodies' submission to it, to its *settled*, routine, and definitive existence. The established apparatus configures space such that the configuration itself remains in the background, as a pure given. From this it follows that what the apparatus brings into existence doesn't appear as having been made *by it*. In this way, the turnstile apparatus meant to stop "fare evasion" *produces* the predicate "evader" rather than preventing fare evasion. THE APPARATUS MATERIALLY PRODUCES A GIVEN BODY AS THE SUBJECT OF THE DESIRED PREDICATE.

The fact that each being, as a *determined* being, is now produced by apparatuses represents a new paradigm of power. In *Abnormal*, Foucault takes the plague-stricken town as the historical model of this new power, of the productive power of apparatuses. It is therefore within administrative monarchies themselves that the form of power which was to supplant them was first exploited; a form of power that no longer operates through exclusion but through inclusion, no longer through public execution but therapeutic punishment, no longer through arbitrary taxation but vital maximization, no longer through personal sovereignty but the impersonal application of faceless norms. The emblem of this transfer of power, according to Foucault, is the *management* of plague-victims as opposed to the *banishment* of lepers. Indeed, plague-victims are not excluded from the town, relegated to an outside, as lepers were. Instead, the plague offers the opportunity to deploy a whole interlinked machinery, a whole systematized distribution, an immense architecture of surveillance, identification, and selection apparatuses. The town, Foucault says, "was divided up into districts, the districts were divided into quarters, and then the streets within these quarters were isolated. In each street there were overseers, in each quarter inspectors, in each district someone in charge of the district, and in the town itself either someone was nominated as governor or the deputy mayor was given supplementary powers when plague broke out. There is, then, an analysis of the territory into its smallest elements and across this territory the organization of a power that is continuous […] a power that was continuous not only in this pyramidal, hierarchical structure, but also in its exercise, since surveillance had to be exercised uninterruptedly. The sentries had to be constantly on watch at the end of the streets, and twice a day the inspectors of the quarters and districts had to make their inspection in such a way that nothing that happened in the town could escape their gaze. And everything thus observed had to be permanently recorded by means of this kind of visual examination and by entering all information in big registers. At the start of the quarantine, in fact, all citizens present in the town had to give their name. The names were entered in a series of registers. […] Every day the inspectors had to visit every house, stopping outside and summoning the occupants. Each individual was assigned a window in which he had to appear, and when his name was called he had to present himself at the window, it being understood that if he failed to appear it had to be because he was in bed, and if he was in bed he was ill, and if he was ill he was dangerous and so intervention was called for." What Foucault describes here is how a paleo-apparatus, the anti-plague apparatus, worked; its essence was, much more than fighting the plague, to produce this or that body *as plague-stricken*. With apparatuses, then, we pass from "a technology of power that drives out, excludes, banishes, marginalizes, and represses, to a fundamentally positive power that fashions, observes, knows, and multiplies itself on the basis of its own effects. [A] power that does not act by separating into large confused masses, but by distributing according to differential individualities."[26]

The West's dualism has long consisted in establishing two antagonistic entities: the divine and the worldly, subject and object, reason and madness, soul and flesh, good and evil, life and death, being and nothingness, etc., etc. The latter established, civilization developed as the struggle of one against the other. This was an exceedingly costly way of going about things. Empire clearly proceeds differently. It still deals in these dualities, *but it no longer believes in them*. In fact, it merely *uses* each couple of classical metaphysics with the purpose of maintaining order, that is: as a binary machine. By apparatus, one should therefore understand a space polarized by a false antimony such that everything that passes through it and happens within it is *reducible* to one or the other of its terms. In this regard, the most immense apparatus ever created was obviously the East-West geostrategic macro-apparatus, which opposed term for term the "socialist bloc" and the "capitalist bloc." Every rebellion, every alterity that happened to appear *anywhere* either had to pledge allegiance to one of these two sides or would find itself unwittingly thrown into the official enemy camp of the power it challenged. One can gauge the violence of currents running through apparatuses, and the incredible noxiousness of Western metaphysics in its decay, by the staying power of the Stalinist rhetoric of "you're playing X's game"—Le Pen's,[27] the right's, globalization's, it doesn't matter—which is but a reflexive transposition of the old rhetoric of "class against class." A geopolitical commonplace involves mocking these "Third-World" Marxist-Leninist ex-guerillas who, since the fall of the East-West macro-apparatus, are supposed to have reformed themselves into mere mafias or adopted an ideology which the gentleman of the Rue Saint-Guillaume[28] consider deranged simply because they fail to understand its vocabulary. In fact, what is now emerging is rather the intolerable effect of the reduction, obstruction, for-matting, and disciplining that every apparatus brings to bear on the *untamed anomaly* of phenomena. *A posteriori*, national liberation struggles look less like stratagems of the USSR than the stratagem of *some-thing else*, something which mistrusts the system of representation and refuses to play a part in it.

What must be understood, in fact, is that every apparatus functions starting from a *couple*—con-versely, experience shows that a couple that *functions* is a couple that *is an apparatus*. A couple, and not a pair or double, for every couple is asymmetrical, includes a major and a minor premise. The major and minor premises are not only nominally distinct—

two "contrary" terms can perfectly designate the same property, and in a sense that is most often the case—they name two *different modalities of aggregating phenomena.* Within the apparatus, the major premise is the norm. The apparatus aggregates what is compatible with the norm through the simple fact *of not distinguishing,* of leaving it submerged in the anonymous mass that upholds what is "normal." Thus, in a movie theater, whoever doesn't scream, or hum, or undresses, etc., remains indistinct, incorporated into the welcoming crowd of spectators, *signifying insofar as insignificant,* short of any recognition. The minor premise of the apparatus is therefore *the abnormal.* That is what the apparatus brings into existence, singles out, isolates, recognizes, differentiates, then reintegrates, *but as disintegrated, separated, different from the rest of the phenomena.* Here we have the minor premise, composed of the whole of what the apparatus individuates, predicates, and in so doing, disintegrates, spectralizes, suspends; a whole, then, that THEY make sure never condenses, never *finds its way,* nor ever conspires. This is where the elementary mechanism of Biopower feeds directly into the logic of representation such as it dominates Western metaphysics.

The logic of representation aims at *reducing* all alterity, effacing what is *there,* what comes into presence, in its pure haecceity, what *makes one think.* All alterity, all radical difference, according to the logic of representation, is apprehended as a negation of the Same, the latter posited by this same logic to begin with. That which differs abruptly, and which thus has nothing in common with the Same, is therefore reduced, projected onto a common plane *which doesn't exist* and within which a contradiction now appears, one of whose terms the Same fears. In the apparatus, that which is not the norm is consequently defined as its negation, as *abnormal*. That which is only *other* is reintegrated as *other than the norm*, as that which *opposes* the norm. The medical apparatus will in this way bring the "sick" into existence as that which *is not well*; the educational apparatus the "good-for-nothing" as that which *is not obedient*; the legal apparatus "crime" as that which *is not legal*. Within the biopolitical, that which is not normal will thus be presented as pathological, when we know from experience that pathology is itself *a norm of life* for the sick organism and that health is not linked to a particular norm of life but to a state of *robust normativity*, to an ability to confront and to create *other* norms of life. The essence of every apparatus is to impose an authoritarian distribution of the sensible in which everything that comes into presence is confronted with the threat of its binarity.

The formidable aspect of every *apparatus* is that it is built around the original structure of human presence:

to which we are called, *summoned* by the world. All our "qualities," our "specific being" are established within a play among beings [*étants*] such that our *disposition* towards beings is not primary. Nonetheless, within the most banal of apparatuses, like a boozy Saturday night among suburban petit bourgeois couples, it often happens that we experience the characteristic, not request, but *possession*, and even the extreme *possessiveness* involved with every apparatus. And it is during the vacuous conversations punctuating the dreadful dinner party that we experience it. One of the Blooms "present" will launch into his tirade against perpetually-on-strike-government-workers; once performed (the role being well known), a counter-polarization of the social-democratic type will issue from one of the other Blooms, who will play his part more or less convincingly, etc., etc. Throughout, these aren't bodies speaking to each other, but rather *an apparatus functioning*. Each of the protagonists sets in motion the series of ready-to-use signifying machines, which are always-already inscribed in *common* language, in grammar, in metaphysics, in the THEY. The only gratification that we can take from this kind of *exercise* is to have performed in the apparatus with some panache. *Virtuosity is the only freedom—a pathetic freedom—gained by submitting to signifying determinisms.*

Whoever speaks, acts, "lives" in an apparatus is in some way *justified* by it. He is made the author of his acts, his words, his behavior. The apparatus ensures the integration, the conversion into an *identity* of a heterogeneous collection of discourses, gestures, attitudes: haecceities. It is by reducing every event to an identity that apparatuses impose a local tyrannical order on the global chaos of Empire. The production of differences, of subjectivities, is also governed by the binary imperative: imperial pacification depends entirely on the production of false antinomies, on the production of simulated conflicts: "For or against Milosevic," "For or against Saddam Hussein," "For or against violence"… Galvanizing these antinomies produces the Bloomifying effect with which we are so familiar; in the end it secures from us the omnilateral indifference on which the full-bore intervention of the imperial police relies. This—the utter astonishment produced by impeccable acting, by the autonomous life, by the artistic machinery of apparatuses and significations—is what we experience in watching any televised debate, if the actors have any talent. In this way, the "anti-globalization" crowd will pit their predictable arguments against "neoliberal" ones. The "unions" will forever replay 1936 facing an eternal Comité des Forges. The police will fight scum. "Fanatics" will face off against the "democrats." The cult of disease will think it is challenging the cult of health. And all the binary unrest will only go to further ensure world slumber. This is how, day after day, THEY carefully spare us the painful obligation to exist.

Janet, who a century ago studied all the precursors of Bloom, consecrated a tome to what he called "psychological automatism." In it, he focuses on all the positive forms of the crisis of presence: suggestion, sleepwalking, obsession, hypnosis, mediumism, automatic writing, psychological disintegration, hallucination, possession, etc. He traces the cause, or rather the *condition* of all these heterogeneous symptoms to what he calls "psychological misery." By "psychological misery" he means a generalized, inextricably physical and metaphysical, weakness of being, which is akin to what we call *Bloom*. This state of weakness, he observes, also provides the conditions for a cure, in particular through hypnosis. The more Blooomified the subject, the more open he is to suggestion and, thus, curable. And the more he recovers, the less effective the medicine, the less suggestible he is. Bloom is therefore the operating condition of apparatuses; Bloom is our vulnerability to them. But contrary to suggestion, the apparatus never aims at some kind of recovery, but rather to become part of us, an indispensable prosthesis to our presence, like a *natural* crutch. There is a need for the apparatus, which the latter satisfies only in order to intensify it. As the undertakers at CNRS would put it, apparatuses "encourage the expression of individual differences."

We must learn to keep ourselves out of sight, to pass unnoticed into the gray band of each apparatus, to *camouflage* ourselves behind its major premise. Even if our first instinct is to oppose a proclivity for the abnormal with the desire for conformity, we have to develop the art of becoming perfectly anonymous, of offering the appearance of pure conformity. We have to develop the pure art of the surface *in order to conduct our operations*. This means, for example, that we must drop the pseudo-transgression of no less pseudo-social conventions, stop opting for revolutionary "sincerity," "truth," and "scandal," for the sake of a tyrannical politeness through which to keep the apparatus and its possessed at bay. *Calling for* transgression, monstrosity, abnormality is the most insidious trap that apparatuses set. Wanting to be—that is, wanting to be unique—within an apparatus is our *principal weakness*. Because of it we remain held, entangled, by the apparatus.. Conversely, the desire *to be controlled*, so frequent among our contemporaries, primarily represents the latter's *desire to be*. For us, this same desire would instead be the desire to be mad, or monstrous, or criminal. But this is the very desire through which THEY control and neutralize us. Devereux has shown that every culture holds a *model negation*, a marked-out exit, for those who want to escape, an outlet that allows the culture to harness the driving force behind every transgression into a higher-order stabilization. Among the Malay, this is called *amok*, in the West, schizophrenia. The Malay is "preconditioned—perhaps unwittingly but certainly quite automatically—by Malay culture to react to almost any violent inner or outer stress by running *amok*. In the same sense, Occidental man of today is conditioned by his own culture to react to any state of stress by schizophrenia-like behavior... [I]n our society, being schizophrenic is the 'proper' way of being 'mad'" (*Schizophrenia: An Ethnic Psychosis, or Schizophrenia without Tears*).[29]

RULE NO. 1 Every apparatus produces singularity in the form of monstrosity. This is how the apparatus reinforces itself.

RULE NO. 2 One never breaks free of an apparatus by engaging with its minor premise.

RULE NO. 3 When THEY predicate you, subjectivate you, summon you, never react and above all never deny anything. For the counter-subjectivation THEY would then force from you forms the prison from which you will *always* have the hardest time escaping.

RULE NO. 4 Greater freedom does not lie in the absence of a predicate, in anonymity *by default*. Greater freedom results instead from the *saturation* of predicates, from their anarchical accumulation. Overpredication automatically cancels itself out in permanent unpredictability. "When we no longer have any secrets, we no longer have anything to hide. It is we who have become a secret, it is we who are hidden" (Deleuze-Parnet, *Dialogues*).[30]

RULE NO. 5 Counter-attack is never a response, but the establishment of a new order.

7

> *[T]he possible implies the corresponding reality with,*
> *moreover, something added, since the possible is the com-*
> *bined effect of reality once it has appeared and of a con-*
> *dition [dispositif] which throws it back in time.*
> — Bergson, *The Creative Mind* [31]

Apparatuses and Bloom co-determine each other like two poles interdependent with the epochal suspension. Nothing ever happens in an apparatus. Nothing ever happens, that is, EVERYTHING THAT EXISTS IN AN APPARATUS EXISTS IN IT AS A POSSIBILITY. Apparatuses even have the power to dissolve an event that has actually occurred—one THEY call a "catastrophe," for example—into its possibility. When a defective airliner explodes in midflight and straightaway THEY deploy a whole panoply of apparatuses which THEY keep running with facts, background stories, declarations, statistics that reduce the event of the death of several hundred people to the status of an *accident*. In no time at all they will have erased the obvious fact that the invention of railroads was necessarily also the invention of railroad catastrophes; and the invention of the Concord the invention of its midflight explosion. THEY thus separate that which belongs to the *essence* of "progress" from that which rightly belongs to its *accident*. And the latter, in the face of all the evidence, THEY throw out. After a few weeks THEY will have reduced the event of the crash to its *possibility*, to its statistical eventuality. From then on the crash will no longer have happened, ITS POSSIBILITY—NATURALLY INFINITESIMAL—HAS BEEN MADE A REALITY. In a word, nothing happened: the essence of technological progress has escaped unharmed. The colossal, composite, signifying monument, which THEY will have constructed for the occasion, realizes here the objective of every apparatus: *maintaining the phenomenal order*. For such is the purpose, within Empire, of every apparatus: *to run and to govern a certain plane of phenomenality, to ensure that a certain economy of presence persists*, to maintain the epochal suspension in the space allocated to it. Hence the strikingly absent, lethargic character of existence within apparatuses, this Bloomesque feeling of being carried away by the comforting flow of phenomena.

We are saying that the mode of being of all things, within the apparatus, is *possibility*. Possibility can be distinguished, on the one hand, from an act and, on the other hand, from power [*puissance*]. Power, in the activity of writing this text, is language, language as the generic ability to signify, to communicate. Possibility is language, that is, the set of utterances considered correct according to French syntax, grammar, and vocabulary as they currently exist.

The act is speech, the enunciation, the production here and now of a particular utterance. Unlike power, possibility is always the possibility of something. *Within the apparatus, everything exists as a possibility* means that everything that occurs in the apparatus occurs *as the actualization of a possibility that preceded it* and that as such is MORE REAL. Every act, every event, is thus reduced to its possibility and emerges within the apparatus as a predictable consequence, as a pure contingency, of its possibility. What happens isn't more real for having happened. This is how the apparatus excludes the event, and excludes it *in the form of an inclusion*; for example, by declaring it possible afterwards.

What apparatuses accomplish is only the most notorious of the impostures of Western metaphysics, which is summed up in the adage "essence precedes existence." For metaphysics, existence is but a predicate of essence; for that matter, every existent is supposed to do nothing more than actualize an essence that supposedly comes first. According to this preposterous doctrine, possibility, that is, the *idea of things* would precede things; every reality would be a possibility *that has, in addition, acquired existence.* When this way of thinking is put right side up, one finds that it is the fully developed reality of a thing whose possibility is postulated *in the past*. Of course, an event has had to happen in the totality of its determinations in order to isolate certain of them, in order to extract the representation of these determinations that will make the event appear as *having been possible*. "The possible," says Bergson, "is only the real with an act of mind which throws its image back into the past once it has been enacted."[32] "To the extent that the possible is open to 'realization,'" adds Deleuze, "it is understood as an image of the real, while the real is supposed to resemble the possible. That is why it is difficult to understand what existence adds to the concept when all it does is double like with like. Such is the defect of the possible: a defect which serves to condemn it as produced after the fact, as retroactively fabricated in the image of that which resembles it."[33]

Everything that is, in an apparatus, is referred either to the norm or to the accident. As long as the apparatus holds, nothing can occur within it. The event, *this act that keeps its power [puissance] within itself,* can come only from outside, as that which demolishes the very thing that should keep it at bay. When noise music burst on the scene, THEY said: "That's not music." When '68 irrupted, THEY said: "That's not political." When '77 had Italy by the throat, THEY said: "That's not Communism." Faced with the old Artaud, THEY said: "That's not literature." Then, when the event lasts, THEY say: "Well, it was possible, it's *one* possibility for music, for politics, for

Communism, for literature." And finally, after the initial moment of shock brought about by the inexorable *work of power* [*puissance*], the apparatus reforms itself: THEY include, defuse, and remap the event; they ascribe it to a possibility, to a *local* possibility—that of the literary apparatus, for example. The jackasses at CNRS, who handle language with such casuistic caution, conclude delicately: "If the apparatus [*dispositif*] prepares for something and makes it possible, that still doesn't guarantee its actualization. It simply gives life to a particular space in which 'something' can occur." THEY couldn't have been clearer.

If the imperial perspective had a slogan it would be "ALL POWER TO THE APPARATUSES!" It is true that in the coming insurrection it will most often suffice to liquidate the apparatuses sustaining enemies in order to break them, enemies that in times past would have had to be shot. At bottom, the slogan has less to do with cybernetic utopianism than with imperial pragmatism: the fictions of metaphysics, these grand barren constructions which now compel neither faith nor admiration, are no longer able to unify the debris of universal disintegration. Under Empire, the old Institutions are deteriorating one after the other in a cascade of apparatuses. What is happening, and what is the truly imperial mission, is the concerted demolition of each Institution into a multiplicity of apparatuses, into an arborescence of relative and unpredictable norms. The educational system, for example, no longer bothers to present itself as a coherent order. It is now but a hodgepodge of classes, schedules, subjects, buildings, departments, programs, and projects that are so many apparatuses meant to keep bodies immobilized. With the imperial extinction of every event thus comes the world-wide, managed dissemination of apparatuses. Many voices can now be heard lamenting such a dreadful age. Some denounce a pervasive "loss of meaning," while others, the optimists, swear every morning to "give meaning" to this or that misery only, invari-ably, to fail. All, in fact, agree to *want meaning with-out wanting the event*. They seem not to notice that apparatuses are by nature hostile to meaning, whose absence it is their job to maintain. *All those who speak of "meaning" without giving themselves the means to upend apparatuses are our direct enemies.* Giving one-self the means sometimes entails only renouncing the comfort of Bloomesque isolation. Most appara-tuses are indeed vulnerable to collective insubordi-nation of whatever kind, not having been designed to withstand it. Just a few years ago, a dozen deter-mined people in a union or welfare office was enough to extort right then and there a thousand francs worth of aid per person who signed up. And today hardly more people are needed in order to carry out an "autoreduction"[34] at the supermarket.

The separation of bodies, the atomization of forms-of-life are the subsistence conditions of most imperial apparatuses. Today, "to want meaning" immediately implies the three stages we have already mentioned, and necessarily leads to insurrection. On this side of the zones of opacity, then of insurrection, there is only the reign of apparatuses, the desolate empire of machines producing *meaning, infusing meaning* in everything that passes through them according to the system of representations locally in effect.

Some people, who consider themselves particularly clever—the same who had to ask a century and a half ago what Communism *would be like*—today ask us what our so-called "reunion on the other side of sig-nifications" might look like. Is it really necessary that so many bodies have never known abandon, the exhilaration of sharing, familiar contact with other bodies, or perfect peace of mind for this kind of ques-tion to be asked with such a knowing air? And, indeed, what point could there be in the event, in striking out meanings, and in ruining their systematic correlations for those who have not carried out the ek-static conversion of attention? What could letting-be mean, the destruction of what stands between us and things, for those who have never noticed the *solicitation* of the world? How could they understand the reason-less existence [*existence sans pourquoi*] of the world, those who are incapable of living without reasons? Will we be strong and numerous enough in the coming insurrection to create rhythms that prevent apparatuses from forming again, from assimilating that which in fact happens? Will we be silent enough to find the pressure point and the scansion that guarantee a veritable pogo effect? Will we know how to harmonize our actions with the pulse of power [*puissance*], with the fluidity of phenomena?

In a sense, the revolutionary question is now a *musical* one.

TRANSLATOR'S NOTES

The endnotes that follow are not part of the original Tiqqun text but have been added by me. In bibliographic references, where no translator is given for a cited French text, the translation is my own.

This Is Not a Program

1. Bruno Bertini, Paolo Franchi, Ugo Spagnoli, and Paolo Bufalni, *Terrorisme et démocratie* (Paris: Editions Sociales, 1978).

2. Tiqqun uses here and frequently elsewhere in the text the French indefinite subject pronoun *on* in all capitals. In general, the pronoun may be translated "we," "one," "you," "they," depending on the context. When it appears in all capitals, I have translated it throughout as "THEY," although the reader should bear in mind the indeterminacy that the pronoun carries in French.

3. Ernst Von Salomon, *The Outlaws*, trans. Ian F. D. Morrow (London: J. Cape, 1931), 233.

4. See Tiqqun, *Théorie du Bloom* (Theory of Bloom) (Paris: La Fabrique, 2004).

5. Michel Foucault, "Intellectuals and Power (A Conversation between Michel Foucault and Gilles Deleuze)," *Language, Counter-Memory, Practice: Selected Essays and Interviews by Michel Foucault*, ed. and trans. Donald F. Bouchard and Sherry Simon (Ithaca: Cornell University Press, 1977), 217.

6. Félix Guattari, "Preface," in Bruno Giorgini, *Que sont mes amis devenus?* (Paris: Sevelli, 1978), 5–6.

7. José Bové, the prominent French agri-unionist, eco-alter-globalizationist and 2007 presidential candidate.

8. *L'encyclopédie des Nuisances* was a revue, published from 1984 to 1992, dedicated to social critique in the vein of the Internationale Situationiste. As an extension of the revue, a publishing house of the same name was created in 1992 and continues to publish.

9. Karl Marx, "A Contribution to the Critique of Hegel's Philosophy of Right: Introduction," *Marx: Early Political Writings*, ed. and trans. Joseph J. O'Malley (Cambridge: Cambridge University Press, 1994), 69.

10. GP, Gauche prolétarienne; PC-MLF, Parti communiste-marxiste-léniniste de France; UJC-ml, Union des jeunes communists-marxistes-léninistes; JCR, Jeunesse communiste révolutionnaire.

11. MLS, Movimento dei Lavoratori per il Socialismo.

12. Franz Kafka, *The Castle*, trans. Anthea Bell (Oxford: Oxford World's Classics, 2009), 46.

13. G. W. F. Friedrich Hegel, *Elements of the Philosophy of Right*, ed. Allen W. Wood, trans. H. B. Nisbet (Cambridge: Cambridge University Press, 1991), 266.

14. The Trotskyist-oriented Socialisme par en bas (Socialism from below) was founded in 1997, following a split in Socialisme international.

15. (Paris: Athropos, 1977), 13.

16. Confederazione Generale Italiana del Lavoro.

17. Michel Foucault, *The History of Sexuality, Vol. 1: An Introduction* (published in French as *La Volonté de savoir*), trans. Robert Hurley (New York: Vintage Books, 1990), 96.

18. Herbert Marcuse, "The Concept of Negation in the Dialectic," *Telos* (Summer, 1971): 130–132.

19. Georges Bataille, "The Psychological Structure of Fascism," trans. Carl R. Lovitt, *New German Critique*, 16 (1979): 65, 67–68, 70, 85.

20. Michel Foucault, "On Popular Justice: A Discussion with Maoists," trans. John Mepham, *Power/Knowledge: Selected Interviews and Other Writings, 1972–1977* (New York: Pantheon Books, 1980), 27. Translation modified.

21. Michel Foucault, "Powers and Strategies," trans. Colin Gordon, ibid., 137–138.

22. Paul Virno, "Do You Remember Counterrevolution?" trans. Michael Hardt, *Radical Thought in Italy: A Potential Politics*, eds. Sandra Buckley, Michael Hardt and Brian Massumi (Minneapolis: University of Minnesota Press, 2006), 244.

23. Maurizio Lazzarato, Yann Moulier-Boutang, Antonio Negri and Giancarlo Santilli, *Des entreprises pas comme les autres: Benetton en Italie, le Sentier à Paris* (Paris: Publisud, 1993).

24. Nanni Balestrini and Primo Moroni, *L'Orda d'Oro. 1968–1977: la grande ondata rivoluzionaria e creativa, politica ed esistenziale* (Milan: Feltrinelli, 1997).

25. Lao Tzu, *Tao Te Ching*, trans. Jonathan Star (New York: Tarcher/Penguin, 2001), 58.

26. "The Black September Action in Munich: Regarding the Strategy for Anti-Imperialist Struggle," *The Red Army Faction: A Documentary History. Projectiles for the People*, eds. and trans. André Moncourt and J. Smith (Montreal: Kersplebedeb Publishing; Oakland, CA: PM Press, 2009), 222.

27. Cynthia Ghorra-Gobin, *Les États-Unis entre local et mondial* (Paris: Presses de Sciences Po, 2000).

28. Tiqqun's precision.

29. Sergio Morandini and Gabriele Martignoni, eds., *Il diritto all'odio. Dentro/fuori/ai bordi dell'area dell'autonomia* (Verona: Bertani editore, 1977). Translated from Tiqqun's French translation.

30. Georges Bataille, "En marge d'*Acéphale*," *Œuvres completes*, tome II (Paris: Gallimard, 1972), 275.

31. Pierre Clastres, "Sorrows of the Savage Warrior," *Archeology of Violence*, trans. Jeanine Herman (New York: Semiotext(e), 1994), 185–186. Translation modified.

32. Ibid., 193.

33. Cesare Battisti, *L'ultimo sparo: un "delinquente comune" nella guerriglia urbana* (Rome: Derive/Approdi, 1998). Translated from Tiqqun's French translation.

34. Frank Kitson, *Low Intensity Operations: Subversion, Insurgency and Peacekeeping* (Harrisburg, Pennsylvania: Stackpole Books, 1971), 49.

35. Lucio Dalla, "Come è profondo il mare," *Come è profondo il mare* (Sony/BMG Italy, 1998 [1977]).

36. Roger Trinquier, *Le Temps perdu* (Paris: Albin Michel, 1978).

37. Roger Trinquier, *Modern Warfare: A French View of Counter-insurgency*, trans. Daniel Lee (New York: Praeger, 2006 [1964]), 18, 19. Translation modified.

38. Johns Biggs-Davison, RUSI Seminar (April 4, 1973), quoted in Carol Ackroyd, Karen Margolis, Jonathan Rosenhead, and Tim Shallice, *The Technology of Political Control* (Harmondsworth: Penguin, 1977), 115.

39. Frank Kitson, op. cit., 2, 201.

40. Translated from Tiqqun's French translation. The text in Italian may be found at the following website: http://www.sindominio.net /laboratorio/documentos/77/excepcion.htm.

41. Tiqqun refers to a TGI (Tribunal de grande instance), one of several types of civil courts in France.

42. Félix Guattari, "Why Italy?" trans. John Johnston, *Autonomia: Post-Political Politics* (Los Angeles: Semiotext(e), 1980), 234.

43. Aelius Aristides, *To Rome*, trans. S. Levin (Glencoe, Illinois, 1950). Quoted in *Roman Civilization: Selected Readings*, eds. Naphtali Lewis and Meyer Reinhold (New York: Columbia University Press, 1990), 58.

44. Luc Boltanski and Eve Chiapello, *The New Spirit of Capitalism*, trans. Gregory Elliot (New York: Verso, 2005), 191.

45. Eric Alliez, Bruno Karsenti, Maurizio Lazzarato and Anne Querrin, "Le pouvoir et la résistance," *Multitudes* 1 (March 2000).

46. Maurizio Lazzarato, "Du biopouvoir à la biopolitique," *Multitudes* 1 (March 2000).

47. Aaron Starobinski, *La Biopolitique, essai d'interprétation de l'histoire de l'humanité et des civilisations* (Geneva: Imprimerie des Arts, 1960).

48. Marie-José Mondzain, *Image, Icon, Economy*, trans. Rico Franses (Stanford: Stanford University Press, 2005), 15, 21, 63. Translation modified.

49. Michael Hardt and Antonio Negri, *Empire* (Cambridge: Harvard University Press, 2000), 413.

50. Georges Henein, "Biopolitique," *Petite Encyclopédie Politique* (Paris: Editions du Seuil, 1969), 28.

51. *Manuale di sopravvivenza* (Bari: Dedalo libri, 1974). Translated from Tiqqun's French translation.

52. The ideology of José Bové. See note 7.

53. ATTAC, *Tout sur ATTAC* (Paris: Mille et une nuits, 2002).

54. Jean de Maillard, *Le Marché fait sa loi: De l'usage du crime par la mondialisation* (Paris: Mille et une nuits, 2001), 119–120.

55. Yann Moulier-Boutang, "Pour un nouveau New Deal," *Chimères* 33 (Spring 1998).

56. Frank Kitson, op. cit., 87.

57. French economist who has written extensively on "existence income."

58. Roger Trinquier, ibid., 7. Quoted in Frank Kitson, op. cit., 29.

59. Gopal Balakrishnan, "Virgilian Visions," *New Left Review* 5 (September–October 2000): 147.

60. Fabrizio Calvi, *Camarade P. 38* (Paris: Grasset, 1982).

61. Marie Dominique-Vergez, Didier Mazover, Gilbert Longhi and Maryse Vaillant, *Face aux incivilités scolaires, quelles alternatives au tout sécuritaire?* (Paris: Syros, 2001).

62. See Tiqqun, *Premiers matériaux pour une théorie de la Jeune-Fille* (Paris: Fayard, 2001).

63. In French, "Chorale de la Fin Du Travail," the capital letters alluding to the French trade union the Confédération Française Démocratique du Travail.

64. Antonio Negri, "Sabotage et autovalorisation ouvrière," trans. Yann Moulier-Boutang, *Usines et ouvriers: Figures du nouvel ordre* (Paris: Maspero, 1980), 152.

… As a Science of Apparatuses

1. All endnotes are those of the translator. In the Tiqqun text, the authors indicate the title given by Reiner Schürmann to his contribution to the "Cahiers de l'Herne" volume dedicated to Martin Heidegger (*Martin Heidegger* [Paris: Editions de l'Herne, 1983], 354–368), an article adapted by Schürmann from his *Principe d'anarchie: Heidegger et la question de l'agir* (Paris: Seuil, 1982). The present, modified English translation is taken from *Heidegger on Being and Acting: From Principles to Anarchy*, trans. Christine-Marie Gros (Bloomington, IN: Indiana University Press, 1987), 5–6.

2. See Tiqqun, *Théorie du Bloom* [Theory of Bloom] (Paris: La Fabrique, 2004).

3. Tiqqun uses here and frequently elsewhere in the text the French indefinite subject pronoun *on* in all capitals. In general, the pronoun may be translated "we," "one," "you," "they," depending on the context. When it appears in all capitals, I have translated it throughout as "THEY," although the reader should bear in mind the indeterminacy that the pronoun carries in French.

4. Ernesto De Martino, *The World of Magic*, trans. Paul Saye White (New York: Pyramid Communications, 1972). Translation modified.

5. See Tiqqun's *Théorie de la jeune fille* (Theory of the Young Girl) (Paris: Fayard, 2001).

6. *From Principles to Anarchy*, op. cit.

7. The French word is *autoroute*, whose translation as "highway" obviously does not capture the *auto-*, "automobile" and "self," "self-same," etc., of the French highway.

8. The RATP (Régie autonome des transports parisiens) is the public authority operating the Parisian public transportation network.

9. *Esprit Libre* refers to the motto of the French bank BNP Parisbas's campaign to market its services to 18–24 year-olds.

10. Centre National de la Recherche Scientifique (National Center for Scientific Research).

11. Hugues Peeters and Philippe Charlier, "Contributions à une théorie du dispositif," *Hermès* 25, "Le dispositif: entre usage et concept," 1999, p. 18–19.

12. Harvard Project on the City, "Shopping," in *Mutations* (Bordeaux: Arc en rêve centre d'architecture; Barcelona: ACTAR, 2000), 140.

13. Hugues Peeters and Philippe Charlier, op. cit.

14. Ludwig Wittgenstein, *Tractatus Logico-Philosophicus*, trans. C. K. Ogden (New York: Routledge, 2005), 79 (§4.1212).

15. Tiqqun writes, "Le dire n'est pas le dit." The English translation of the passage, taken from Martin Heidegger, *Contributions to Philosophy (From Enowning)*, trans. Parvis Emad and Kenneth May (Indiana Univ. Press, 1999), 4, reads "This saying [that of the "thinking-saying of philosophy"] does not describe or explain, does not proclaim or teach. This saying does not stand over against what is said. Rather, the saying itself *is* the 'to be said,' as the essential swaying of being."

16. Gilles Deleuze, "Dires et profils," in *Poésie* 36 (December 1947): 68–78.

17. G.W.F. Hegel, *Phenomenology of Spirit*, trans. A.V. Miller (Oxford: Oxford University Press, 1977), 60.

18. Ludwig Wittgenstein, *On Certainty*, trans. G. E. M. Anscombe and G. H. Writght (Oxford: Blackwell Publishing, 1975), 77e.

19. Translation of "Le dispositif: une aide aux identités en crise?" the title of an essay by Annabelle Klein and Jean-Luc Brackelaire in *Hermès* 25, op. cit., 67–81.

20. Michel Foucault, *Archeology of Knowledge*, trans. A. M. Sheridan Smith (New York: Pantheon Books, 1971), 131.

21. The reference is to Georg Lukàcs's 1962 preface to *The Theory of the Novel*: "A considerable part of the German intelligentsia, including Adorno, have taken up residence in the 'Grand Hotel Abyss' […] 'a beautiful hotel, equipped with every comfort, on the edge of an abyss, of nothingness, of absurdity. And the daily contemplation of the abyss between excellent meals or artistic entertainments, can only heighten the enjoyment of the subtle comforts offered.'" Trans. Anna Bostock (Cambridge, MA: MIT Press, 1971), 22.

22. Karl Marx, *Capital: Volume 1*, trans. Ben Fowkes (New York: Penguin Classics, 1990), 173.

23. Review founded by Gilles Deleuze and Félix Guattari in 1987. "Negrist" refers to an adherent of Antonio Negri's brand of Marxist political philosophy.

24. Ernesto De Martino, *The World of Magic*, op. cit. Translation modified.

25. Hugues Peeters and Philippe Charlier, op. cit., 20.

26. Michel Foucault, *Abnormal: Lectures at the Collège de France 1974–1975*, trans. Graham Burchell (New York: Picador, 2004), 45–46, 48.

27. Jean-Marie Le Pen, founder and former head of the far-right French political party the Front National (FN).

28. The Rue Saint-Guillaume in Paris is the location of the university Institut d'études politiques (Institute of Political Science).

29. Included as Chapter 10 in George Devereux, *Basic Problems of Ethnopsychiatry*, trans. Basia Miller Gulati and George Devereux (Chicago: The University of Chicago Press, 1980), 218, 220.

30. Gilles Deleuze and Claire Parnet, *Dialogues*, trans. Hugh Tomlinson and Barbara Habberjam. (New York: Columbia University Press, 1987), 46. Translation modified.

31. Henri Bergson, *The Creative Mind*, trans. Mabelle L. Andison (New York: The Citadel Press, 1992), 101.

32. Ibid., 100.

33. Gilles Deleuze, *Difference and Repetition*, trans. Paul Patton (New York: Columbia University Press, 1994), 212.

34. A practice associated with Italian and French autonomist movements, autoreduction (*autoréduction*) is a direct action by which one refuses to pay for public transport, gas, food, or other goods or services. After announcing as much, the *autoréducteur* simply—and politically—takes what he cannot afford, effectively reducing prices to zero.

semiotext(e) intervention series